TOP 10
NEW ENGLAND

PATRICIA HARRIS
& DAVID LYON

EYEWITNESS TRAVEL

Left **State House, Providence, Rhode Island** Right **Winter landscape, Killington, Vermont**

LONDON, NEW YORK,
MELBOURNE, MUNICH AND DELHI
www.dk.com

Produced by Coppermill Books
55 Salop Road London E17 7HS
Printed and bound in China
by South China Printing Co.

First American Edition, 2010

12 13 14 15 10 9 8 7 6 5 4 3 2 1

Published in the United States by:
Dorling Kindersley Limited, 80 Strand,
London WC2R 0RL, UK
**Copyright, 2010, 2012 © Dorling
Kindersley Limited, London
Reprinted with revisions 2012**

ISSN 1479-344X
ISBN 978-0-7566-8543-0

Within each Top 10 list in this book,
no hierarchy of quality or popularity
is implied. All 10 are, in the editor's opinion, of
roughly equal merit.

MIX
Paper from
responsible sources
FSC   FSC™ C018179
www.fsc.org

Contents

New England's Top 10

The information in this DK Eyewitness Top 10 Travel Guide is checked regularly.
Every effort has been made to ensure that this book is as up-to-date as possible at the time of
going to press. Some details, however, such as telephone numbers, opening hours, prices,
gallery hanging arrangements and travel information are liable to change. The publishers
cannot accept responsibility for any consequences arising from the use of this book, nor for
any material on third-party websites, and cannot guarantee that any website address in this
book will be a suitable source of travel information. We value the views and suggestions of
our readers very highly. Please write to: Publisher, DK Eyewitness Travel Guides, Dorling
Kindersley, 80 Strand, London WC2R 0RL, UK, or email: travelguides@dk.com.

Left **Boston Red Sox v. Kansas City Royals, Fenway Park** Right **Fall foliage, New Hampshire**

Left **Portland Head Light, Cape Elizabeth, Maine** Right **Mount Tom Park, Litchfield, Connecticut**

NEW ENGLAND'S TOP 10

NEW ENGLAND'S TOP 10

TOP10 New England's Highlights

New England is six states rolled into one amazing, all-season destination of pine-scented mountains, briny ocean villages, sophisticated urban centers – and so much more. It's also the birthplace of America, a fact attested by a multitude of historic homes and museums. Icons abound: covered bridges, snowy ski slopes, blazing fall foliage, lighthouses perched on craggy cliffs, white churches on town greens, and tail-flapping lobsters fresh from the sea.

Historic Boston 1
The American past is palpable in New England's largest city, where cobbled streets echo with the calls of patriots, restaurants and shops enliven an ancient granite market, and the Freedom Trail unites momentous sites *(see pp8–9)*.

2 Mount Desert Island, Maine
Rugged headlands above a crashing ocean, pine forests crisscrossed with hiking trails, and still ponds reflecting the sky's blue bowl express nature in all its unbounded wildness *(see pp10–11)*.

Cape Cod, Massachusetts 3
The bent arm of Cape Cod is a summer world of untamed dunes, bird-filled marshes, and quirky towns where you can savor fresh fish, sticky taffy, and the salt tang of sea breezes *(see pp12–13)*.

Newport
Lake Champlain
St Johnsbury
Berlin
Rangeley
Burlington
VERMONT
Montpelier
Lincoln
5 White Mountains
Middlebury
Green River
Green Mountains 7
Hanover
Lakes Region 9
NEW HAMPSHIRE
Manchester
Concord
Portsmouth
Manchester
Brattleboro
Lowell
Williamstown
Concord
Pittsfield
MASSACHUSETTS
1 Boston
Berkshires 10
Springfield
Worcester
Providence
Litchfield Hills 6
Hartford
RHODE ISLAND
CONNECTICUT
4 Newport
Mystic
New Haven

50 — miles — 0 — km — 50

4 Newport, Rhode Island
Opulent mansions on seaside cliffs reveal the splendors of the Gilded Age in one of America's most storied yachting harbors *(see pp14–15)*.

➔ Preceding pages **Covered bridge at West Arlington, Vermont**

White Mountains, New Hampshire

Summer hikers and winter skiers relish these rugged granite mountains cloaked in alpine forest. Hike, drive, or ride the cog railway up Mount Washington, the northeast's tallest peak *(see pp16–17)*.

Litchfield Hills, Connecticut

Bistros, bakeries, and boutiques often fill the historic white clapboard buildings of hill-country villages in this region where artists, actors, and authors keep their country home retreats *(see pp18–19)*.

Green Mountains, Vermont

From pre-Revolutionary villages to ridgeline hiking trails, the Green Mountains form the spine of Vermont. In fall, its forests blaze with color; in winter, some of the nation's top slopes lure skiers *(see pp20–21)*.

Portland, Maine, and Casco Bay

Maine's largest city remains a seafaring center on a picturesque bay, but the Old Port's handsome brick blocks also host taverns, galleries, and boutiques *(see pp22–3)*.

Lakes Region, New Hampshire

With its shoreline of 240 miles (386 km), Lake Winnipesaukee rules New Hampshire's kingdom of mountain-rimmed lakes. Fishing, boating, and waterskiing make the region a summer playground *(see pp24–5)*.

Berkshires, Massachusetts

Theater, music, and dance flourish in the gentle Berkshire Hills, where lavish estates of a bygone era's millionaires lend a sophisticated air to homespun country villages *(see pp26–7)*.

TOP 10 Historic Boston

Founded in 1630 by Puritans who envisioned their settlement as a shining beacon to the world, Boston was among America's first great urban centers. Its patriots led the rebellion that grew into the American Revolution, and few places in the US evoke so vividly the birth of a nation. Centuries later, Boston remains at the national forefront in politics, the arts, culture, education, and science. The city retains its Classical proportions and human scale, with modern buildings nudging up against landmarks of the Colonial and Revolutionary eras.

Massachusetts State House

⭐ As you might expect, security is tight at the USS *Constitution*. Don't carry anything you couldn't take on an airplane.

🍴 The food court at Quincy Market, adjacent to Faneuil Hall, offers good variety and value for a quick lunch.

Top 10 Features

1 Massachusetts State House
2 Boston Common and Public Garden
3 African Meeting House
4 Granary Burying Grounds
5 Fenway Park
6 Faneuil Hall
7 Old North Church
8 USS *Constitution*
9 Paul Revere House
10 Harvard Yard

Massachusetts State House
Completed in 1798, this legislative temple with its ornate marble and paneled halls, was architect Charles Bulfinch's masterpiece, and the model for capitols around the country.

Boston Common and Public Garden
Concerts, rallies, and Shakespeare plays enliven the Common, Boston's green heart since 1634. Tens of thousands of flowers bloom in the Public Garden, while on its pond fantastical Swan Boats glide.

African Meeting House
At the African Meeting House and adjacent Abiel Smith School you'll catch an intimate glimpse of the African-American experience, from slavery to abolition.

Granary Burying Grounds
Visit the graves of some of Boston's most famous characters at this Tremont Street graveyard *(left)* of more than 2,300 slate tombstones planted in the shadow of downtown skyscrapers.

Fenny Park

Fenway Park
Whatever their loyalties, baseball fans hope to see a game in Fenway before they die. Opened in 1912, it's the oldest Major League Baseball park, and a shrine to the national pastime.

Faneuil Hall
One of Boston's most significant Revolutionary sites, Faneuil Hall heard firebrands like Samuel Adams *(left)* call the populace to open revolt against the King. Public debates are still staged here among the historical portraits in the Great Hall.

Old North Church
The spare decor and humble box pews typical of a Colonial house of worship barely hint at the fame of Christ Church *(right)*, where lanterns hung in its belfry warned of British invasion of the countryside.

USS *Constitution*
The world's oldest active warship, the three-masted frigate nicknamed "Old Ironsides" *(below)* has served in the US Navy since 1797, battling North African pirates and foreign navies alike.

Paul Revere House
Revere's house, built around 1680, is the oldest in Boston. Get an intimate look at the domestic life of this key figure in the history of the American Revolution.

Harvard Yard
Free student-led tours through Harvard Yard *(left)* provide insight into life at America's first and most prestigious university, founded in 1636. Touch the foot of the John Harvard statue for luck.

This Way to History

The Freedom Trail (a red line on the pavement, either paint or bricks) snakes through Boston to highlight 16 important sites of Colonial and Revolutionary history. The 2.5-mile (4-km) walking trail begins at Boston Common and ends with climbing Bunker Hill Monument in Charlestown. Pick up a map and inquire about free, ranger-led Freedom Trail tours at the Boston National Historical Park information center at Faneuil Hall. (617 242 5642, www.nps.gov/bost).

New England's Top 10

⊤10 Mount Desert Island, Maine

Mount Desert Island condenses the fabled Maine coast and woods into a single magical spot. Salt-splashed fishing villages dot the southwest lobe, while Bar Harbor, on the east, bustles with restaurants and lodging options. Painters of the 19th-century Hudson River School were among the first to celebrate Mount Desert's wild natural beauty, and their art encouraged wealthy industrialists to build summer estates thoughtfully incorporated into natural settings. Half the island falls within Acadia National Park.

Bar Harbor

🅒 **Acadia National Park is one of the most visited parks in the National Park system. For summer visits, reserve lodgings far in advance.**

🅠 **Check out Trenton Bridge Lobster Pound (see p122).**

• Map R3
• Acadia National Park Visitor Center: off Rte. 3, Hulls Cove; 207 288 3338, 877 444 6777 (camping reservations); open mid-Apr–Jun: 8am–4:30pm daily; Jul–Aug: 8am–6pm daily; Sep: 8am–5pm daily; adm; www.nps.gov/acad
• Jordan Pond House: Park Loop Rd., Seal Harbor; 207 276 3316; open 11am–9pm mid-May–late Oct; www.jordanpond.com
• Abbe Museum: 26 Mount Desert St., Bar Harbor; 207 288 3519; open late May–early Nov: 10am–5pm daily; winter: 10am–4pm Thu–Sat; adm; www.abbemuseum.org

Top 10 Features

1. Bar Harbor
2. Cadillac Mountain
3. Thunder Hole
4. Jordan Pond House
5. Sand Beach
6. Abbe Museum
7. Carriage Roads
8. Southwest Harbor
9. Bass Harbor Head and Lighthouse
10. Hiking Trails

Cadillac Mountain

It's worth rising *very* early to hike or drive up 1,527-ft (465-m) Cadillac Mountain *(above)* to catch the first rays of the sun to strike the US. Lay-a-beds should plan on savoring amazing panoramas at sunset.

Thunder Hole

Swift tides and wind-whipped waves pounding the craggy ledges at Thunder Hole force air and water into a deep crease beneath the rock. Under the right conditions, spectators are rattled by a ground-shaking thunderclap coming from the hole.

Bar Harbor

Grand mansions still line the shore of this lively resort town on Frenchman Bay. Bar Harbor functions as a tourist center for the island. It's also a convenient base for visiting Acadia National Park or taking a schooner cruise *(see p121)*.

Jordan Pond House

For a touch of gentility in the wilderness, nothing beats sitting in Adirondack chairs on the grassy lawn of the Jordan Pond House, where you can enjoy their famous popovers with afternoon tea. The restaurant also serves lunch and dinner.

⇒ *The 27-mile (43-km) Loop Road takes in highlights of the coast and the hilly uplands. Trailhead parking lets you explore further on foot.*

10 Newport, Rhode Island

This small city packs an amazing amount of history into a few square miles. Not only does it boast America's first naval college and first synagogue, its White Horse Tavern has been pulling pints since 1673. In the late 1800s, the super-rich began building ornate mansions along the cliffs south of the city center to escape fetid summers in New York. The New York Yacht Club made Newport its summer headquarters, and the city's harbor is home to many contenders for the America's Cup, the most prestigious match race in sailing.

Exterior of The Breakers

🅐 An inexpensive RIPTA trolley day pass is the best and most economical way to see Newport.

🅒 Look for a truck selling Del's Lemonade along Thames Street or at Fort Adams State Park.

• Map F5
• Newport Visitor Information Center: 23 America's Cup Ave.; 401 845 9123; open daily
• The Breakers: 44 Ochre Point Ave.; 401 847 1000; open daily; adm
• International Tennis Hall of Fame: 194 Bellevue Ave.; 401 849 3990; open daily; adm
• America's Cup Charters cruises; 401 846 9886; open May–Oct; adm
• Rose Island Lighthouse; 401 847 4242; open daily July–Labor Day
• Museum of Yachting: Fort Adams State Park; 401 847 1018; open Wed–Mon Jun–Oct; adm
• Fort Adams State Park: Harrison Ave.; 401 847 2400; open daily; free
• Touro Synagogue: 85 Touro St; 401 847 4794; call for tour schedule; adm

Top 10 Features

1. The Breakers
2. Cliff Walk
3. International Tennis Hall of Fame
4. America's Cup Charters Cruises
5. Rose Island and Lighthouse
6. Museum of Yachting
7. Fort Adams State Park
8. Touro Synagogue
9. Washington Square
10. Bowen's Wharf

1 The Breakers

Once you've toured the gilt- and marble-encrusted interior of this 70-room Italian Renaissance-style mansion completed in 1895, you'll have an appreciation of the preeminence of the Vanderbilt family – who called it home – among America's economic aristocracy.

3 International Tennis Hall of Fame

Play tennis on the grass courts where American tournament tennis was born in 1881 (below). The Hall still hosts the only US professional matches played on grass, and its museum chronicles 800 years of tennis history.

2 Cliff Walk

The exhilarating amble (above) along Newport's east-facing cliffs will have you looking two ways at once — up to the back lawns of the mansions on Bellevue Avenue and down to watch surfers catching waves at Easton's Beach.

5 Sand Beach

Rugged cliffs and jumbled ledges line most of Acadia's shoreline, but thousands of visitors flock to this 870-ft (265-m) stretch of sandy cove (above) to sunbathe. Swimming is bracing, as the ocean water rarely exceeds 55° F (15° C).

6 Abbe Museum

Explore 10,000 years of Native-American culture in this 50,000-item collection devoted to the heritage of Maine's Wabanaki peoples (right). In summer, see demonstrations of basketry and wood-carving.

7 Carriage Roads

To preserve a state of auto-free tranquillity, John D. Rockefeller Jr. constructed 45 miles (72 km) of carriage roads (below) through land that he donated to Acadia National Park. They are still reserved for hikers, cyclists, cross-country skiers, and equestrians.

8 Southwest Harbor

A snug harbor tucked inside two lobes of Mount Desert Island, picturesque Southwest Harbor is the tranquil alternative to Bar Harbor. Take a lobster-hauling boat ride or catch the Cranberry Isles ferry here (see p121).

10 Hiking Trails

To penetrate the deep wilderness or get up close and personal with the mountains of Acadia National Park, use the network of more than 120 miles (193 km) of trails. They range from easy to extremely strenuous.

9 Bass Harbor Head and Lighthouse

At the southern tip of Mount Desert, Bass Harbor Head (main image) towers above the sea on the ruptured face of a continental plate. From the lighthouse you'll be gripped by panoramas of sky and deep blue ocean.

Acadia National Park was created in 1919, then vastly expanded with tracts donated by John D. Rockefeller Jr.

11

TOP 10 Cape Cod, Massachusetts

When you reach Race Point at the tip of Cape Cod, you might feel you've come to the end of the earth. Beyond this long, thin crook of glacial sand lies the broad Atlantic, stretching all the way to Portugal. The Cape's fishing fleets haul the sweetest scallops and richest tuna; virtually every cove harbors a hamlet founded by farmers whose grandchildren turned to the sea. Its beaches extend for 30 miles (48 km), from Chatham to Provincetown, comfortably accommodating the thousands of swimmers and sunbathers who flock here.

Cape Cod Canal

◉ If you're traveling with children, drive Rte. 28 to enjoy its rich array of mini-golf courses, ice cream stands, and other diversions for the "are-we-there-yet?" set.

◉ Kream 'N Kone (Rtes. 28 and 134, West Dennis; 508 394 0808) serves some of Cape Cod's best fried seafood.

• Cape Cod Welcome Center: Jct. Rtes. 6 and 132, Hyannis; Map H4; 508 362 3225; open daily during summer
• Nickerson State Park: Rte. 6A, Brewster; Map H4; 508 896 3491, 877 422 6762 (camping reservations); open daily; park: free; camping: adm; www.mass.gov/dcr/parks/southeast/nick.htm
• Cape Cod National Seashore Salt Pond Visitor Center: Rte. 6, Eastham; Map H4; 508 255 3421; open daily Sep–Jun: 9am–4:30pm; Jul–Aug: 9am–5pm; adm (beach and parking); www.nps.gov/caco

Top 10 Features

1. Cape Cod Canal
2. Sandwich Boardwalk and Town Beach
3. King's Highway
4. Nickerson State Park
5. Cape Cod Rail Trail
6. Falmouth and Woods Hole
7. Hyannis
8. Chatham
9. Cape Cod National Seashore Beaches
10. Provincetown

1 Cape Cod Canal
Dug to save ships from the treacherous Nantucket Shoals, the canal marks the Cape's sedate beginning. Pedal the bike paths or cast a line from the banks for striped bass and ferocious bluefish.

2 Sandwich Boardwalk and Town Beach
Songbirds whistle as you clip-clop over Great Marsh on the Sandwich Boardwalk *(right)*. The gentle waves and warm waters of Cape Cod Bay make Town Beach ideal for small children.

3 King's Highway
More shady lane than highway, Route 6A strings together the salty Cape Cod Bay villages filled with the mansions of Victorian sea captains, antiques dealers, and the studios of potters, glassblowers, and other artisans.

4 Nickerson State Park

Eight crystal-clear glacial kettle ponds dot this wooded parkland far removed, both physically and ecologically, from the Cape Cod seashores. Watch rare songbirds, canoe and fish the ponds *(left)*, and camp at more than 420 sites.

5 Cape Cod Rail Trail
One of the most invigorating ways to see Cape Cod, the trail begins in Dennis, crosses fields and forest, skirts a quaint fishing harbor, and follows dune cliffs into Wellfleet.

6 Falmouth and Woods Hole
Marine researchers dominate tiny Woods Hole, a harbor of professors who look like pirates. Falmouth proper is a quintessential New England town of neat houses and tall churches.

7 Hyannis
Hyannis is Cape Cod's market town and transportation hub, thanks to its airport and two ferry lines that shuttle back and forth to Nantucket and Martha's Vineyard.

8 Chatham
An iconic lighthouse marks the dangerous shoals off Chatham's astounding and ever-shifting barrier beaches *(above)*, where seabirds flock and seals bask in the winter sun. Home to the Cape's main tuna fleet, Chatham is also a yachtsmen's harbor.

9 Cape Cod National Seashore Beaches
When glaciers receded 15,000 years ago, they left behind a vast swath of fine sand hammered by relentless waves. Beaches for swimming, kite-flyers, surfers, and sunbathers stretch the way from Nauset Beach to Race Point with its historic Life Saving Station

10 Provincetown
It's always party time in P-town *(right)*. The Cape's most colorful community is at once a Portuguese-American fishing village, a major art colony, and a leading gay resort destination.

14

4 America's Cup Charters Cruises

Enjoy the beauty of Newport Harbor from the deck of a racing yacht that once competed for the America's Cup. You may even get to take the wheel.

5 Rose Island and Lighthouse

Volunteer keepers man this historic lighthouse a mile offshore from Newport. Experienced paddlers often kayak to the island for excellent birding.

6 Museum of Yachting

Located at Fort Adams (below), this fascinating facility tells the story of yacht racing in Newport. Photographs, replica miniatures, and trophies fill the galleries. Classic yachts float outside.

7 Fort Adams State Park

The windy point between Newport Harbor and the Narragansett Bay East Passage is perfect for watching racing sailboats or flying kites. Newport's famous jazz and folk festivals are held here.

9 Washington Square

Colonial-era Newport's focal point was damaged but not destroyed by British occupiers during the American Revolution. The city's oldest house (1697) stands nearby.

8 Touro Synagogue

The oldest synagogue in the country, spare and elegant Touro Synagogue was constructed in 1763 by religious refugees from Spain and Portugal. Its services still follow Sephardic rites.

Bowen's Wharf 10

You could develop a nautical swagger walking Bowen's Wharf (right), the anchor of Newport's waterfront activity since 1760. Head here for sail or powerboat tours, shopping at retail boutiques, or both casual and fine dining.

Newport Regatta

Usually held in mid-July, the Newport Regatta features racing in more than 20 "One-Design" classes, where boats from all over North America compete against others of like design. It's quite a thrill seeing more than 250 sleek racing vessels straining before the wind, but sailing is only half the fun, as the regatta is the highlight of Newport's summer social season that begins at the marinas and spills out to the restaurants and bars.

America's Cup Charters cruises depart from Newport Harbor Hotel & Marina, 49 America's Cup Ave.

TOP 10 White Mountains, New Hampshire

More than 20 summits topping 4,000 ft (1,200 m) define the rugged north country of New Hampshire, of which 1,200 sq miles (3,116 sq km) is set aside as the White Mountain National Forest. The area is ideal for some of the main outdoor activities of New England: summer hiking and climbing, fall foliage sightseeing, and winter skiing. Drive through the White Mountains to encounter soaring mountain ridges, tumbling waterfalls, deep glens, and dark forests. Wildlife abounds – be careful of deer and moose on the roads at dusk.

Conway Scenic Railroad

In foliage season, drive the "Kanc" on a weekday, when there's less traffic.

Pick up a picnic at Half Baked & Fully Brewed, 187 Main St. (Rte. 112), in Lincoln (603 745 8811).

• Map L3–4, M3–4
• Franconia Notch State Park Flume Gorge & Visitor Center; 603 745 8391; open daily May–Oct; adm
• White Mountain National Forest Saco District Ranger Station: 33 Kancamagus Hwy.; 603 447 5448; open daily
• Mount Washington Cog Railroad: Marshfield Base Station, off Rte. 302; 603 278 5404; open Apr–Dec; adm
• Conway Scenic Railroad: Rte. 16, North Conway; 603 356 5251; mid-Apr–Dec; adm
• Pinkham Notch Visitor Center: Joe Dodge Lodge, Rte. 16, north of North Conway; 603 466 2721; open daily
• North Conway Outlet Malls; www.northconwaynh.com

Top 10 Features

1. Franconia Notch State Park
2. Kancamagus Highway
3. Mount Washington and Mount Washington Cog Railroad
4. Ski Mountains
5. Mount Washington Hotel and Resort
6. Conway Scenic Railroad
7. The Balsams
8. Pinkham Notch
9. Lincoln and Woodstock
10. North Conway

1 Franconia Notch State Park

Stop along this 8-mile (13-km) pass between the Franconia and Kinsman mountain ranges to walk the narrow-cut Flume Gorge *(below)* with its dramatic steep rock walls and gushing waterfalls. Challenging hiking trails cut through the park.

2 Kancamagus Highway

One of few roads crossing the spine of the White Mountains, the 26.5-mile (43-km) "Kanc" is among the state's most thrilling drives. Park the car and get out at the designated scenic areas to picnic, hike, or explore Colonial history.

For more on places to see foliage See pp36–7

3 Mount Washington and Mount Washington Cog Railroad

New England's highest peak at 6,288 ft (1,917 m), Mount Washington has lured climbers and sightseers since the 1840s. For the most picturesque ascent, take the Cog Railway, operating since 1869.

4 Ski Mountains

Precipitous drops and heavy snowfall make the White Mountains a top ski destination. Cannon Mountain *(see p55)* and development-free Wildcat Mountain also have extensive summer activities. Loon Mountain boasts major mountain-biking trails.

5 Mount Washington Hotel and Resort

Legendary golfing and invigorating winter skiing are just two of the draws to this palatial resort, which opened in 1902. It remains the queen of the old-time White Mountains resorts.

6 Conway Scenic Railroad

See the scenery as earlier generations did – from a train. Go through Mount Washington Valley, or over the towering trestles and cliffside rails of Crawford Notch.

7 The Balsams

Nestled on a lake in a photogenic valley at the northern edge of the White Mountains, The Balsams *(above)* looks like a fairytale compound. Steeped in history, it has been a near-wilderness getaway since 1866.

8 Pinkham Notch

This rocky mountain pass is the White Mountains hub for hikers and backcountry skiers. Hikes range widely from easy walking *(below)* to challenging expert trails in Tuckerman Ravine.

10 North Conway

Gateway to the east side of the White Mountains, North Conway is a bustling commercial center. Spend the morning hiking, and the afternoon cruising for discounted designer goods at more than 200 outlet stores.

9 Lincoln and Woodstock

With the Kancamagus Highway to the east and Franconia Notch to the north, Lincoln and Woodstock are the civilized little villages that serve as easy-going base camps for hikers, climbers, and skiers.

For more on Mount Washington Hotel and Resort **See p148**
For more on The Balsams **See p146**

Litchfield Hills, Connecticut

Tucked into the northwest corner of Connecticut, the undulating Litchfield Hills are the most scenic and bucolic section of the state. Technically an extension of the Taconic Mountains and the Berkshire Hills, the region is laced with a network of icy-cold mountain streams, making fly-fishing for trout a leading springtime activity. Most sizable towns nestle in the valley of the Housatonic River, and their historic homes and gardens attest both to Colonial settlement and more recent gentrification by wealthy New Yorkers.

Woodbury Antiques sign

🌲 **Visit the gardens of White Flower Farm (167 Litchfield Rd., Morris; 800 503 9624) on Rte. 63 south of Litchfield.**

🍴 **Dine on barbecued meats at the Cookhouse in New Milford *(see p95).***

- Map B4, B5
- Kent Falls State Park: Rte. 7, Kent; 860 927 3238; open daily; adm
- Institute for American Indian Studies: 38 Curtis Rd., Washington; 860 868 0518; open daily; adm
- Shepaug Dam Bald Eagle Observation Area: River Rd., Southbury; 800 368 8954; open late Dec–mid-Mar; free (reservations required)
- Farmington River Tubing: 92 Main St., New Hartford; 860 693 6465; open late May–early Sep; adm
- Lime Rock Park: 60 White Hollow Rd., Lakeville; 860 435 5000; open Apr–Oct; adm
- Mount Tom State Park: Rte. 202, Litchfield; 860 567 8870; open daily; adm

Top 10 Features

1. Litchfield
2. Kent Falls State Park
3. Institute for American Indian Studies
4. Woodbury
5. Shepaug Dam
6. Farmington River Tubing
7. Lime Rock Park
8. Lake Waramaug
9. Housatonic River
10. Mount Tom State Park

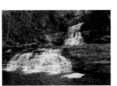

Kent Falls State Park

North of the art-gallery-filled village of Kent, this park is home to Connecticut's most impressive waterfall *(above)*, a 200-ft (61-m) drop over slate and marble. Follow the trail to the top to see the most vigorous chute of all.

Institute for American Indian Studies

Tucked high into the hilly woods of Washington, this facility re-creates a pre-European-contact Algonkian village *(below)*. With artifacts dating back 10,000 years, it's the perfect spot to learn about the woodlands culture of northwestern Connecticut.

Litchfield

Local gentry flock to this market town to shop, dine, and worship. Litchfield is filled with historic homes, including the first US law school (1784).

Woodbury

Join collectors and interior decorators as they scour Woodbury's 40-plus antiques dealers. Check out late-18th-century style at the historic Glebe House *(see p92).*

5 Shepaug Dam

In icy winter, more bald eagles congregate at the Shepaug Dam in Southbury than almost any other place in New England. Camouflaged blinds let birdwatchers get closeup views of the magnificent raptors catching fish.

6 Farmington River Tubing

Chill out on a hot summer day by floating down the Farmington River on an inflatable tube. The 2.5-mile (4-km) course includes gentle ripples, a short segment of turbulent rapids, and a lot of indolent floating.

7 Lime Rock Park

The air is charged with testosterone and motor fumes at Lime Rock auto-racing track. Races range from stock cars to road racers to formula vehicles. High-speed driving classes are offered.

8 Lake Waramaug

Farmland around New Preston's Lake Waramaug is temperate enough to grow wine grapes. Stop by Hopkins Vineyard *(above)* to sample the wines. A state park on the broad, scenic lake offers picnic grounds and swimming.

Neighbors with Names

The combination of Litchfield Hills' rural beauty and the region's easy proximity to New York City conspire to make it the home of many celebrities. Among the residents over the years have been sculptor Alexander Calder, author William Styron, chef Jacques Pepin, and a number of entertainers, including actress Meryl Streep.

10 Mount Tom State Park

Views from the summit of Mount Tom entice hikers to climb this modest peak – an elevation gain of only 500 ft (152 m). The park's lake is a favorite with scuba divers and family swimming parties alike.

9 Housatonic River

As the Housatonic River *(above)* approaches the covered bridge at West Cornwall, it enters a 12-mile (19-km) stretch that many rank the best fly-fishing in the eastern US. Join sportsmen from around New England here in the spring.

TOP10 Green Mountains, Vermont

These mountains form the backbone of Vermont, running north-south from the Massachusetts border to Quebec, between the Champlain and Connecticut River valleys. Much of this stunning wilderness is set aside as the Green Mountain National Forest, which draws millions of visitors in every season for fishing, hiking, mountain biking, camping, canoeing, skiing, and snowshoeing. State Route 100, which runs between the east and west ranges of the Green Mountains, is among the most striking roads in the country for fall foliage.

Fall colors on the Mount Equinox Skyline Drive

⭐ Especially in the north, temperatures plummet in winter, spelling icy conditions. Be prepared for road closings.

☕ The Warren Store (Main St., Warren) has hot grilled food, some sandwiches, as well as pastries and sweets at breakfast and lunch.

• Map K3–6
• Green Mtn. National Forest Manchester Ranger Station: 2538 Depot St., Manchester Center; 802 362 2307; open Mon–Fri; free
• Bennington Battle Monument: 15 Monument Circle, Bennington; 802 447 0550; open daily mid-Apr–Oct; adm
• Hildene: 1005 Hildene Rd., Manchester; 802 362 1788; open daily; adm
• Green Mtn. Club Visitor Center: 4711 Waterbury-Stowe Rd.; 802 244 7037; open late May–mid-Oct: daily; mid-Oct–late May: Mon–Fri; free

Top 10 Features

1. Bennington
2. Manchester
3. Mount Equinox Skyline Drive
4. Hildene
5. Killington
6. Robert Frost Wayside
7. Middlebury
8. Mad River Valley
9. The Long Trail
10. Stowe and Mount Mansfield

1 Bennington

The Bennington Battle Monument *(above)* commemorates a major American Revolutionary War victory and provides sweeping panoramas of this southwest corner of the Green Mountains. The Bennington Museum *(see p102)* displays important folk art and Americana.

2 Manchester

A genteel vacation resort since the 1890s, Manchester *(below)* is so posh that its sidewalks are marble. Shop in the upscale designer outlet stores on the outskirts, or hit the slopes at nearby Stratton and Bromley ski areas.

3 Mount Equinox Skyline Drive

This 5-mile (8-km) toll road, along a high ridge, offers spectacular sunsets and breathtaking views of the Green, White, Adirondack, Berkshire, and Taconic mountain ranges in Vermont, New York, New Hampshire, and Massachusetts.

4 Hildene

This 24-room Georgian Revival mansion *(above)* was built for Robert Todd Lincoln (1843–1926), diplomat son of President Abraham Lincoln (1809–65). It features family memorabilia and a 1,000-pipe Aeolian organ. Formal gardens crown the impressive grounds.

5 Killington

At 4,235 ft (1,290 m), Killington *(left)* is the second highest peak in the Green Mountains. It is also home to the largest ski and snowboard resort in eastern North America *(see p55)*.

6 Robert Frost Wayside

Poet Robert Frost (1874–1963) and the Vermont landscape where he farmed are inseparable. See nature through a poet's eyes by following the interpretive trail in Ripton to a cabin where he wrote his verse.

9 The Long Trail

This 270-mile (432-km) path follows the Green Mountains from Massachusetts to Quebec, crossing most of Vermont's highest peaks. Take a day hike between access points.

8 Mad River Valley

Tucked between two ranges of the Green Mountains, this region boasts a ski area *(see p55)*, chic Waitsfield village, and the outdoors sports center of Warren. Historic covered bridges cross many streams.

7 Middlebury

Prestigious Middlebury College brings sophistication to this archetypal New England community of Colonial homes and pointy-spired churches *(above)*. Visit the old mill buildings along Otter Creek, Vermont's longest river, for a photogenic waterfall and a cluster of shops and boutiques.

10 Stowe and Mount Mansfield

The Von Trapps of *Sound of Music* fame settled in Stowe *(right)* because it so resembled the Austrian Alps. Hikers and skiers flock to the village at the foot of Vermont's tallest peak, 4,393-ft (1,339-m) Mount Mansfield.

For more on Robert Frost **See p101**

21

🔟 Portland, Maine, and Casco Bay

There's good reason that the motto of Maine's largest city is Resurgam, or "I shall rise again." Portland has burned down four times since its foundation in 1633. Building codes set up after the Great Fire of 1866 created a legacy of handsome Victorian structures. Recent redevelopment has transformed the waterfront with dining and entertainment amid the working docks, and former warehouses have become the boutiques and galleries of the Old Port District. A short drive from downtown lie the parks and sandy beaches of Casco Bay.

Portland Schooner

🦋 Be prepared for some steep walking, often on cobbles or bricks. Residential Portland occupies a high ridge; downtown sits on the steep slope down to the water.

🔵 Get great snacks and meals at Public Market House (28 Monument Sq., Portland; 207 228 2056).

• Map N4
• Odyssey Whale Watch: 170 Commercial St.; 207 775 0727 • Maine Sailing Adventures: Maine State Pier, Commercial St.; 207 749 9169 • Children's Museum and Theatre of Maine: 142 Free St.; 207 828 1234 • Portland Head Light & Fort Williams State Park: Shore Rd., Cape Elizabeth; 207 799 2661 • Crescent Beach State Park: Rte. 77, Cape Elizabeth; 207 799 5871 • Two Lights State Park: off Rte. 77, Cape Elizabeth; 207 799 5871; • Portland Sea Dogs: 271 Park Ave.; 800 936 3647

Top 10 Features
1. Old Port District
2. Western Promenade
3. Portland Museum of Art
4. Victoria Mansion
5. Whale Watch and Windjammer Cruises
6. Children's Museum and Theatre of Maine
7. Portland Head Light and Fort Williams Park
8. Crescent Beach State Park
9. Two Lights State Park
10. Portland Sea Dogs

Old Port District
The colorful, jaunty shops of the Old Port District range from dealers in antiques and fine crafts to coffee roasters, clothing boutiques, and candy stores. Both fresh-caught lobsters and harbor island commuters come ashore at the docks.

Western Promenade
Ogle the Victorian mansions in the West End *(right)* en route to the Western Promenade, designed by the Olmsted company famed for New York's Central Park. Views from the landscaped clifftop reach all the way to the White Mountains.

3 Portland Museum of Art
Set in a complex of three historic buildings, the museum features painters of the Maine landscape, notably Winslow Homer (1836–1910), Marsden Hartley (1877–1943), and Rockwell Kent (1882–1971).

4 Victoria Mansion
Portland-born hotelier Sylvester Morse (1816–93) made his fortune in New Orleans. The elaborate Italianate manse *(left)* which he built in 1860 as a summer home certainly showed the folks back home how well he'd done.

7 Portland Head Light and Fort Williams Park
Maine's oldest lighthouse, Portland Head *(above)* was erected in 1791 as part of Fort Williams. The fort is in ruins, but the stately beacon marking the entrance to Casco Bay remains one of the most photographed lighthouses in the world.

10 Portland Sea Dogs
A minor-league affiliate of major-league baseball's Boston Red Sox, the Sea Dogs have a loyal, almost fanatical following in Portland. Hadlock Field even mimics the dimensions of Boston's Fenway Park, with the "Maine Monster" left-field wall.

9 Two Lights State Park
Sandy dunes and rocky points intersect at this state park, named for a pair of 19th-century lighthouses. Noted paintings of these by Edward Hopper (1882–1967) helped stop their demolition in the 1980s.

5 Whale Watch and Windjammer Cruises
You can see humpback, finback, and minke whales roll in the water, spout, and even leap during a four-hour whale watch; or view Portland from Casco Bay on a two-hour sail aboard a gaff-rigged sloop.

6 Children's Museum and Theatre of Maine
An ambitious program of plays for children and interactive exhibits that both entertain and enlighten make the Children's Museum and Theatre of Maine *(below)* an essential place to visit with kids up to age 12.

8 Crescent Beach State Park
Spread out a blanket, search for shells, or take a dip to enjoy the soft sand and safe waters at this park *(below)*, favored by Portland locals but little known to travelers.

For more on the Portland Museum of Art **See p44**

📖10 Lakes Region, New Hampshire

Some of New England's most stunning lakes dot the high plateau and foothills just south of the White Mountains. Formed around 12,000 years ago, these waters began attracting settlers in the mid-18th century. Roads and railroads through the area proliferated in the 19th century, opening New Hampshire's lakes to mass tourism. There's something for everyone here, from the honky-tonk strand of Weirs Beach to the stately grace of Wolfeboro; from the tranquillity of Squam Lake to the roaring racetrack in nearby Loudon.

M/S Mount Washington

🎵 Catch free concerts on Saturday nights in July and August at Cate Park bandstand in Wolfeboro.

🍽 For hearty pub dining with great views of Winnipesaukee, try Patrick's Pub & Eatery in Gilford *(see p114)*.

• Map M4, M5
• Lakes Region Association: Exit 20, Tilton; 603 286 8008
• M/S Mount Washington: 211 Lakeside Ave., Weirs Beach; 603 366 5531; open late May–mid-Oct; adm • Gunstock Mountain Resort: 719 Cherry Valley Rd., Gilford; 603 293 4341; open year-round; adm
• Squam Lakes Natural Science Center: Rte. 113, Holderness; 603 968 7194; open daily May–Oct; adm
• Castle in the Clouds: Moultonborough (Rte. 171); 603 476 5900; open daily Jun–mid Oct; adm
• Winnipesaukee Scenic Railroad: 154 Main St., Meredith; 603 279 5253; open May–Oct; adm

Top 10 Features

1. Lake Winnipesaukee
2. Wolfeboro
3. Weirs Beach
4. *M/S Mount Washington*
5. Meredith
6. Gunstock Mountain Resort
7. Ossipee
8. Squam Lake
9. Castle in the Clouds
10. Winnipesaukee Scenic Railroad

Wolfeboro

A resort destination since 1763, when the Royal Governor built a summer home here, Wolfeboro represents the demure, gentrified side of Winnipesaukee. The village is the largest community on the lake.

Weirs Beach

Fun-lovers swarm this brassy resort *(below)* on the west end of Lake Winnipesaukee, where the beach and boardwalk are augmented by fairground rides, a water slide, mini-golf, souvenir shops, and all the cotton candy you can eat.

Lake Winnipesaukee

Swimmers from across the state love to congregate on the pine-clad beaches of this, New Hampshire's largest lake. The more daring also race motorboats and compete at waterskiing.

M/S *Mount Washington*

Cruising the 20-mile (32-km) length of Winnipesaukee on this 230-ft (70-m) historic vessel is the most relaxing way to see the lake; and while you relax, you can listen to a running commentary on celebrity homes and natural attractions along the way.

Meredith

Warm-water bass fishing is one of the lures of upscale Meredith, the epicenter of tasteful resort development on Lake Winnipesaukee. Capitalizing on New Hampshire's lack of sales tax, Meredith is also the lake's premier shopping destination.

Gunstock Mountain Resort

Born as a Depression-era public works project, Gunstock has evolved into a popular family ski area. In the summer, its vast forests *(left)* make the resort a favorite for camping, hiking, mountain biking, and horseback riding.

Ossipee

Enjoy the rural pleasures of hiking, blackberry picking, and horseback riding in the quiet country roads around Ossipee *(below)*, set in a pond-dotted plateau just to the east of Lake Winnipesaukee.

Squam Lake

Best known as the loon-haunted lake of the 1981 movie *On Golden Pond*, Squam *(left)* is a natural paradise, perhaps best appreciated on a boat tour with a guide from the Squam Lakes Natural Science Center.

Winnipesaukee Scenic Railroad

You never lose sight of Winnipesaukee on summer shoreline excursions between Meredith and Lakeport, with stopovers at Weirs Beach. The railroad also operates weekend fall foliage trips from Meredith or Weirs Beach.

Castle in the Clouds

Tour this stone castle *(below)*, set on a bluff 750 ft (229 m) above Lake Winnipesaukee. Then hike the 3-hour loop trail of the grounds, or take a brief stroll to a stunning waterfall.

Motorcycle Week

Motorcycle enthusiasts gather by the tens of thousands in and around Laconia during mid-June for the adrenaline-charged races, touring, and extreme partying of Laconia Motorcycle Week, an annual event since 1925. Area lodging books up well in advance, so make plans accordingly.

Share your travel recommendations on **traveldk.com**

Berkshires, Massachusetts

Colonial-era villages of the southern Berkshires attest to the rich soils of the Housatonic Valley, while former brick mill towns of the north hint at 19th-century industrialization. Today, though, the region's identity revolves around the summer arts scene: music, dance, theater. The natural world, too, is always alluring. Mountain laurel explodes into bloom in June, and deer browse in abandoned apple orchards. Mountaintop trails lead to sweeping views, or you can hike into deep woods where a waterfall plunges into a still pool.

Mount Greylock hiking trail sign

🌀 **If you're looking for an easy climb, try modest Monument Mountain on Rte. 7 a few miles south of Stockbridge. The roundtrip hike to the summit takes about 90 minutes.**

🌀 **Head to the deli behind Rubiner's Cheesemongers (264 Main St., Great Barrington; 413 528 0488) for gourmet sandwiches, many with exotic cheeses.**

• Map B2, B3
• Berkshires Visitors Bureau: 3 Hoosac St., Adams, 413 743 4500; open Mon–Fri
• Mt. Greylock State Reservation Visitor Center: 30 Rockwell Rd., Lanesborough; 413 499 4262; open daily year-round; free

Top 10 Features

1. Lenox
2. Stockbridge
3. Great Barrington
4. Pittsfield
5. Williamstown
6. North Adams
7. Mount Greylock
8. Hancock Shaker Village
9. Tanglewood Music Center
10. Jacob's Pillow Dance Festival

Lenox

A quaint village surrounded by grand houses and vast estates largely built as summer "cottages" between 1880 and 1910, Lenox *(below)* is the epicenter of luxury shopping and the summer performing arts scene.

Stockbridge

American illustrator Norman Rockwell (1894–1978) modeled his nostalgic treatments of rural American life on the people and buildings of this slow-paced village *(right)*, dominated by the Red Lion Inn.

Great Barrington

A vibrant mix of artists, artisans, savvy business folk, and New Age visionaries makes Great Barrington easily the hippest town in the Berkshires, as well as a gateway to antiques shopping on Route 7 south of town.

Pittsfield
The biggest community of the Berkshires has shed its manufacturing past to become a city of the arts. Catch contemporary art in its galleries, popular music in the glorious concert hall, and visionary plays at its theater *(above)*.

Williamstown
Prestigious Williams College *(below)* gives a youthful spirit to this historic village at the edge of Mount Greylock. Don't miss the treasures in the Sterling and Francine Clark Art Institute (now known as The Clark).

Mount Greylock
American authors Nathaniel Hawthorne and Henry David Thoreau climbed Greylock and sang its praises. You can reach the summit, too, either via several scenic hiking trails or by car.

North Adams
This erstwhile factory town *(main image)* at the west end of the Mohawk Trail has embraced the art world and vice versa. Provocative contemporary art fills a former mill at Mass MoCA *(see p45)*.

Hancock Shaker Village
Now a museum *(above)*, Hancock was among the most influential of 19th-century Shaker communities. Its Round Barn is considered to be a masterpiece of vernacular architecture.

Tanglewood Music Center
The summer home of the Boston Symphony Orchestra since 1940, Tanglewood also hosts jazz, chamber music, and popular music concerts, and runs an important music education program.

Jacob's Pillow Dance Festival
This woodsy mountaintop retreat in Becket is the venue for performances by top-flight dance companies from around the world, as well as workshop productions of new choreography.

For more on the Clark Art Institute **See p45** *For more on the Mohawk Trail* **See p36** *For more on Tanglewood* **See p73**

Left **Scenic railroad, Mt. Washington** Center **Pilgrim monument, Plymouth** Right **Yankee clipper**

🔟 Moments in History

1 10000 BC–AD 1000: Settlement

As glaciers retreated from New England some 12,000 years ago, hunters moved in. By AD 1000, they lived in seasonal villages and farming augmented hunting and fishing. Most spoke an Algonkian language; their dialects persist on Native lands in Massachusetts, Maine, and Connecticut.

2 1620: Colonization

Religious reformers from England swarmed into New England; first the Pilgrims, at Plymouth, Massachusetts (1620), then Puritan colonies at Salem (1626) and Boston (1630). Soon communities were springing up in Rhode Island, Connecticut, and New Hampshire.

3 1775: Revolution

Tensions between mother country and colonies came to a head in 1775 with the occupation of Boston. On April 19, British redcoats and American rebels exchanged fire in Lexington and Concord. Within weeks, the American Revolution had begun.

4 1800–60: Whaling Hegemony

In the 1700s, Nantucket Islanders were among the first to hunt whales around the globe. The whale-oil business proved immensely lucrative, justifying

The Death of General Warren at the Battle of Bunker Hill (American Revolution)

larger ships and longer voyages. New Bedford, Massachusetts, was the world capital of whaling from the 1820s until petroleum displaced whale oil in the 1860s.

5 1785: Trade with China

Merchants from Salem opened China to American trade in 1785. By 1845, New England shipbuilders had evolved the Yankee clipper, a swift sailing vessel that dominated the China trade into the 1860s.

Arctic whale hunters, New Bedford, c.1882

6 1861–5: Abolition and the Civil War

New England led the fight to abolish slavery in the United States. The region harbored fugitive slaves, and abolition societies flourished in both black and white communities. New Englanders volunteered in overwhelming numbers to fight for the Union in the Civil War (1861–5), which decimated many rural areas.

7 1799–1821: Industrialization and Manufacturing

From 1799 to 1813, Eli Whitney's Connecticut gun plants pioneered interchangeable parts and the assembly line. In 1821, textile entrepreneurs brought the Industrial Revolution to Lowell, Massachusetts, complete with purloined English loom designs and a factory-city scheme quickly replicated throughout the region.

8 1865–1900: The Gilded Age

In the late 19th century, great wealth was generated as railroads spanned the country, industry expanded exponentially, and immigrants flowed into the country to fill job openings.

9 1890–1950: The Rise of Tourism

Railroad construction opened the mountains and coasts of New England to scenic tourism. After World War II, new highways and roadside motels brought multitudes of new visitors to Cape Cod, the Maine coast, and the White and Green Mountains.

10 1960–Today: Education and the Knowledge Economy

The founding of Harvard College in 1636 gave New England a head start in higher education. The emphasis on scholarship has persisted down the years, producing industrial leaders in such fields as information technology, robotics, and biotechnology.

Harvard University graduation ceremony

Top 10 Reformers and Revolutionaries

1 Dorothea Dix (1802–87)
Advocate for the mentally ill, Dix also led Union Army nursing in the Civil War.

2 William Lloyd Garrison (1805–79)
Garrison edited the radical newspaper *The Liberator* and co-founded the American Anti-Slavery Society.

3 Joseph Smith (1805–44)
This Vermont-born visionary founded Mormonism.

4 Harriet Beecher Stowe (1811–96)
Prominent abolitionist Stowe attacked slavery in her 1852 novel, *Uncle Tom's Cabin*.

5 Clara Barton (1821–1912)
Nurse, teacher, and suffragist, Barton founded the US branch of the International Red Cross.

6 Mary Baker Eddy (1821–1910)
Eddy was the founder of the Christian Science movement.

7 Justice Oliver Wendell Holmes Jr. (1841–1935)
This Supreme Court Justice was noted for his blunt and pithy opinions.

8 W.E.B. DuBois (1868–1963)
Sociologist, scholar, and activist, DuBois was among the 20th century's most prominent civil rights leaders.

9 Benjamin Spock (1903–98)
Pediatrician Spock shook up US child-rearing by emphasizing affection over discipline.

10 Howard Dean (b.1948)
Dean transformed political campaigning in the US by tapping the powers of cyberspace networking.

Left **Billings Farm & Museum** Center **Slater Mill** Right **Cotton mill, Lowell National Historical Park**

Colonial and Historic Sites

1 Old Sturbridge Village, MA

Heritage livestock breeds and costumed guides create a vivid sense of New England rural life in the early 19th century at this living history museum. The village features more than 40 historic buildings moved from across the region. ◊ *Rte. 20, Sturbridge • Map D3 • 508 347 3362 • Open mid-Apr–mid-Oct: 9:30am–5pm daily; mid-Oct–mid-Apr: 9:30am–4pm Tue–Sun • Adm • www.osv.org*

2 Strawbery Banke, NH

Follow the development of Portsmouth, NH, in this complex of historic dwellings assembled at Strawbery Banke, the city's original settlement. Period furnishings and historical gardens help to chronicle the daily life of the seaside city from the 17th to the 20th century. ◊ *14 Hancock St., Portsmouth • Map N6 • 603 433 1100 • Open May–Oct: 10am–5pm daily; Nov–Dec: call for tour hours • Adm • www.strawberybanke.org*

3 Billings Farm & Museum, VT

Set up in 1871, Billings Farm was turned into a museum of rural life in 1982. Its rolling green pastures and fine farm buildings represent the ideal of Vermont dairy farming. Interact with sheep, horses, and chickens, and watch the herd of Jersey cows being milked. ◊ *River Rd., Woodstock • Map K5 • 802 457 2355 • Open May–Oct: 10am–5pm daily; Nov–Feb 10am–3:30pm Sat, Sun • Adm • www.billingsfarm.org*

4 Lowell National Historic Park, MA

Lowell launched the Industrial Revolution in the United States, and this urban park preserves the city's network of canals and many of its 19th-century textile mills. The racket of the mighty water-powered looms operating in the 1864 Boott Cotton Mill gives a real sense of what it was like to work here. ◊ *Map F2 • Visitor Center: 246 Market St, Lowell; 978 970 5000 • Open Mar–Oct: 9am–5pm daily; Nov–Feb: 9am–4:30pm Mon–Sat, 10am–5pm Sun • Adm • www.nps.gov/lowe*

5 Plimoth Plantation, MA

Step back to 1627 at Plimoth Plantation, where costumed interpreters speaking 17th-century English portray original settlers inside the stockaded village so studiously that references to modern life are met with quizzical looks. There are Native American interpreters at the re-created Wampanoag encampment. ◊ *137 Warren Ave., Plymouth • Map G4 • 508 746 1622 • Open late Mar–Nov: 9:30am–5pm daily • Adm • www.plimoth.org*

Plimoth Plantation

6 Canterbury Shaker Village, NH

Founded in 1792, Canterbury was a working Shaker village into the 1960s. Demonstrations and workshops teach you about Shaker skills and ideals, while informative daily tours of original Shaker buildings include fond anecdotes of the sect's final generation. ◈ 288 Shaker Rd., Canterbury • Map M5 • 603 783 9511 •Open mid-May–Oct: 10am–5pm daily; Nov–early Dec: selected weekends • Adm • www.shakers.org

7 Weir Farm National Historic Site, CT

The painter J. Alden Weir (1852–1919) made this rustic farm into a retreat for himself and his friends at the end of the 19th century. Two more generations of artists worked here before the property passed into the care of the National Park Service. ◈ 735 Nod Hill Rd., Wilton • Map B5 • 203 834 1896 • Open May–Oct: 9am–5pm Wed–Sun; Nov–Apr: 10am–4pm Thu–Sun • Free • www.nps.gov/wefa

8 Slater Mill, RI

Dating from 1793, Slater Mill was the first successful cotton-spinning mill in the United States. The ingenuity of the early machinery, which was driven by water power transmitted through giant flapping leather belts, will fascinate engineering buffs. ◈ 67 Roosevelt Ave., Pawtucket • Map E4 • 401 725 8638 • Open Mar–Apr: 11am–3pm Sat–Sun; May–Oct: 10am–4pm Tue–Sun • Adm • www.slatermill.org

9 Hancock Shaker Village, MA

Learn about the artful skills of the Shakers at this settlement founded in 1790. The iconic 1826 Round Stone Barn perfectly encapsulates their penchant for making things both functional and beautiful. ◈ 1843 W. Housatonic St., Rte. 20, Pittsfield • Map B2 • 413 443 0188 • Open mid Apr–late May: 10am–4pm daily; late May–mid-Oct: 10am–5pm daily • Adm • www.hancockshakervillage. org

Minute Man Statue

10 Minute Man National Historical Park, MA

On April 19, 1775, British troops engaged Colonial rebels in Lexington and Concord. This opening salvo of the American Revolution sent the British Army into retreat and galvanized other colonies to take up arms. Exhibits and annual reenactments held here depict a stirring historical moment. ◈ Map F2 • North Bridge Visitor Center: 174 Liberty St., Concord; 978 369 6993 • Open daily (visitor center open daily mid-Mar–Oct: 9am–5pm; Nov: 9am–4pm; Dec–mid-Mar: 11am–3pm) • Free • www.nps.gov/mima

Left **Maine Lighthouse Museum** Center **Submarine** *Nautilus* Right **Maine Maritime Museum**

Maritime Sites

1 Mystic Seaport, CT

Walk the decks of a tall ship, or see carpenters replank a vessel at this "museum of America and the sea." Mystic Seaport replicates a 19th-century coastal village with craftspeople plying their trades, historic vessels, and a working shipyard. ◈ *75 Greenmanville Ave., Mystic • Map D5 • 860 572 0711 • Open Apr–Oct: 9am–5pm daily; Nov: 10am–4pm daily, Dec & mid-Feb–Mar: 10am–4pm Thu–Sun • Adm • www.mysticseaport.org*

2 Maine Maritime Museum, Bath, ME

Ships have been built at the mouth of the Kennebec River for more than three centuries. Here, sail-era artifacts, paintings of historic vessels, and displays of Maine maritime life chronicle both the practicalities and the romance of that trade. ◈ *243 Washington St. • Map P4 • 207 443 1316 • Open 9:30am–5pm daily • Adm • www.mainemaritimemuseum.org*

3 Penobscot Marine Museum, Searsport, ME

Tiny Searsport was home to 10 per cent of America's deep-water sea captains by the close of the 19th century. Recapture the adventure of that time at this museum, with captains' chests from the China Trade, a whale's jaw, and a wall of portraits of some 300 Searsport sea captains. ◈ *5 Church St. • Map Q3 • 207 548 2529 • Open 10am–5pm Mon–Sat, noon–5pm Sun late May–mid-Oct • Adm • www.penobscotmarinemuseum.org*

4 New Bedford Whaling National Historical Park, New Bedford, MA

In the late 19th century, New Bedford was the world's leading whaling port. Many buildings of the era, including the Seamen's Bethel chapel mentioned in Herman Melville's *Moby-Dick*, are preserved at this park. Don't miss the extraordinary scrimshaw carvings and a half-scale whaling ship at the New Bedford Whaling Museum. ◈ *33 William St. • Map F4 • 508 996 4095 • Open 9am–5pm daily • Free • www.nps.gov/nebe*

5 Nantucket Whaling Museum, Nantucket, MA

Partially set in a former whale-oil refinery and candle factory, this museum tells how one small island dominated a lucrative industry for nearly a century. A 46-ft (14-m) sperm whale skeleton suspended from the ceiling sets the tone. ◈ *15 Broad St. • Map H5 • 508 228 1894 • Open mid-May–Oct: 10am–5pm daily; Nov–mid-Dec: 11am–4pm Thu–Mon • Adm • www.nha.org*

Penobscot Marine Museum

6 Maine Lighthouse Museum, Rockland, ME

This is one of the world's largest collections of lighthouse artifacts. Marvel at gigantic prisms that made small lamps visible far out at sea, and learn how keepers lived. ✪ 1 Park Dr. • Map Q3 • 207 594 3301 • Open late May–Oct: 9am–5pm Mon–Fri, 10am–4pm Sat–Sun; Nov–late May: 9am–5pm Thu–Fri, 10am–4pm Sat • Adm • www.mainelighthousemuseum.org

7 Expedition Whydah Sea Lab & Learning Center, Provincetown, MA

"Black Sam" Bellamy went down with his ship in a storm off Cape Cod in April 1717. This dockside display bristles with discoveries from the ongoing excavation of the wreck – including authentic pirate treasure. ✪ 16 MacMillan Wharf • Map H3 • 508 487 8899 • Open daily mid-May, Sep–Oct: 9am–5pm; Jun–Aug: 10am—7pm • Adm • www.whydah.com

8 Salem Maritime National Historic Site, Salem, MA

Salem's merchants brought the riches of the Far East back home. Uncover their story by retracing their steps along the historic wharves.

✪ 193 Derby St. • Map F2 • 978 740 1650 • Open Mar–Nov: 9am–5pm daily; Dec: 1–5pm Tue–Fri, 9am–5pm Sat–Sun; Jan–Feb: 9am–5pm Sat–Sun • Adm • www.nps.gov/sama

9 Historic Ship *Nautilus* and the Submarine Force Museum, Groton, CT

Tour the world's first nuclear-powered vessel and learn about the first submarine to dive 20,000 leagues

Salem Maritime National Historic Site

under the sea. Visitors can try commanding the sub at simulated controls. ✪ 1 Crystal Lake Rd. • Map D5 • 860 694 3174 • Open May–Oct: 9am–5pm Wed–Mon; Nov–Apr: 9am–4pm Wed–Mon • Free • www.ussnautilus.org

10 Lake Champlain Maritime Museum, Vergennes, VT

Relics from the more than 200 ships that have been wrecked on Lake Champlain are displayed here. Full-size working replicas of historic vessels help to bring the lake's boating history alive. ✪ 4472 Basin Harbor Rd. • Map J4 • 802 475 2022 • Open 10am–5pm daily late May–mid-Oct • Adm • www.lcmm.org

For more on Salem See p69

Left **Mt. Greylock seen from Mohawk Trail** Right **Jamaica Pond, in Boston's Emerald Necklace**

Ways to See Foliage

1 White River Flyer, VT
Take a jaunt through the southern Vermont woods aboard vintage railcars pulled by a diesel locomotive for spectacular views of the Connecticut river and some of the deep gorges of its tributaries. In fall, the maple trees blaze with flame-like colors. ◈ *102 Railroad Row, White River Junction • Map K6 • 802 463 3069 • Jul–mid-Oct • Adm • www.rails-vt.com*

2 Mohawk Trail, MA
This historic Indian trade route over the Berkshire Hills follows the upper ranges of the Deerfield River – resplendent with acid-yellow alder and birch – until it climbs through fiery stands of maple, birch, and beech in the Charlemont State Forest. The drive ends by spiraling down the hillsides at the aptly named Hairpin Turn *(see p72).*

3 K-1 Gondola, VT
After a scenic gondola ride to the highest lift-served terrain in Vermont, a short, easy hike brings you to the summit of Killington Peak *(see p55)* for a panoramic view of five states and part of Canada.

4 Kancamagus Highway, NH
Few foliage drives in New England match the thrill of hurtling along the "Kanc" through a tunnel of

Kancamagus Highway

kaleidoscopic colors. Stop along the way to savor the experience by hiking to a waterfall or sunning on mid-stream glacial boulders *(see p16).*

5 Essex Steam Train & Riverboat, CT
Combine a trip through the woods in restored railcars pulled by coal-fired steam locomotives with a cruise on the Connecticut River aboard a three-deck Mississippi-style river-boat. ◈ *Exit 3 off Rte. 9, Essex • Map D5 • 860 767 0103 • May–Dec • Adm • www.essexsteamtrain.com*

K-1 Gondola

6 Route 100, VT
Perhaps New England's ultimate road for leaf-peeping, Route 100 passes natural wonders like Moss Glen Falls, follows the Mad River through several scenic villages, then rises high into the Green Mountains. ◈ *Map K2–6*

7 Lake Champlain Cruise, VT

Hop aboard the *Spirit of Ethan Allen III* for a narrated cruise around Lake Champlain. While adults admire the brightly painted forests that surround the lake, kids might keep an eye out for Champ, the legendary resident sea serpent. ⊗ *Burlington Boathouse, 1 College St., Burlington • Map J3 • 802 862 8300 • mid-May–mid-Oct • Adm • www.soea.com*

8 Deerfield River Rafting, MA

The Deerfield River has some of the most exhilarating rapids and most scenic gorges in New England. Nothing compares to the rush of bankside colors during foliage season. ⊗ *Map C2 • Zoar Outdoor: 800 532 7483; Jun–Sep; adm; www.zoaroutdoor.com*

Mt. Monadnock, popular with hikers

9 Mount Monadnock, NH

The 3,165-ft (965-m) summit of Mount Monadnock offers incredible views. It's especially worth the scramble over boulders in colorful fall foliage season. ⊗ *Off Rte. 124, west of Jaffrey • Map L6 • 603 532 8862 • Sunrise–sunset daily • Adm • www.nhstateparks.org*

10 Boston's Emerald Necklace

Boston is blessed with an almost continuous chain of parks stretching from downtown sky-scrapers to leafy suburbia. In the fall, this 5-mile (8-km) cycle route is an explosion of red, purple, orange, and yellow as the foliage reaches its climax. ⊗ *Map V4, W4*

Top 10 Covered Bridges

1 Bulls Bridge

1842 Town lattice and queenspost over Housatonic. ⊗ *Rte. 7, Kent, CT • Map B4*

2 Cornish-Windsor Bridge

1866 Town lattice, rebuilt in 1989. Spans Connecticut River between New Hampshire and Vermont. ⊗ *Rte. 12A, Plainfield, NH • Map L5*

3 Hemlock Bridge

1857 Paddleford truss over Saco River. ⊗ *Off Rte. 302, Fryeburg, ME • Map M4*

4 Artist's Covered Bridge

1872 Paddleford truss, also known as the Sunday River Bridge. ⊗ *Off Rtes. 2 and 26, Newry, ME • Map N3*

5 Stark Bridge

1862 Paddleford truss. Spans Upper Ammonoosuc River in village center. ⊗ *North Rd, Stark, NH • Map M3*

6 Albany Covered Bridge

1858 altered Paddleford truss. Crosses Swift River. ⊗ *Dugway Rd., off the Kancamagus Hwy., Albany, NH • Map M4*

7 Ashuelot Bridge

1864 Town lattice truss over Ashuelot River. ⊗ *South of Rte. 119, Bolton Rd, Upper Village, Winchester, NH • Map K6*

8 Warren Bridge

Asymmetrical queenspost across Mad River. ⊗ *East of Rte. 100, Warren, VT • Map K4*

9 Paper Mill, Silk, and Henry Bridges

Three bridges dating 1840–2000 cross the Waloomsac River. ⊗ *South of Rte. 67A, Bennington, VT • Map J6*

10 Burkeville Bridge

Howe truss bridge over South River. ⊗ *Rte. 116, Conway, MA • Map C2*

The Town lattice bridge was the brainchild of Connecticut architect Ithiel Town, who patented his innovative design in 1820.

Left **Old Lyme, wetlands** Center **Granite Theatre, Westerly** Right **Wiscasset, village center**

🔟 Villages

Wethersfield, Connecticut

Founded in 1634 as one of Connecticut's original three settlements, Wethersfield remains an enclave of some of the most striking Colonial architecture in the country – though architecture buffs can get equally excited about the distinctive early-20th-century Hubbard Bungalows. Visit the three 18th-century homes of the Webb-Deane-Stevens Museum to understand the roots of the Colonial Revival movement in American style *(see p89)*. ◈ *Webb-Deane-Stevens Museum: 211 Main St., Wethersfield CT: 860 569 0612; open May–Oct; adm; www.webb-deane-stevens.org*

Wiscasset, Maine

A thriving shipbuilding town in the 18th and 19th centuries, Wiscasset immodestly claims to be the "prettiest village in Maine." With baronial sea captains' homes that define the Federal style, a charming waterfront, and a generous sprinkling of boutiques and restaurants, it just might be. The 1807 Nickels-Sortwell House, built for a wealthy ship owner, recaptures Wiscasset's glorious past *(see p118)*. ◈ *Nickels-Sortwell House: 121 Main St., Wiscasset, ME: 207 882 7169; open Jun–mid-Oct; adm; www.historicnewengland.org*

Tiverton Four Corners, Rhode Island

The crossroads center of rural Tiverton on the east side of Narragansett Bay is filled with boutiques, antiques shops, and art galleries set in largely 18th-century buildings. The surrounding countryside is noted for its handsome historical stone walls and pastoral landscapes. The town also boasts an outstanding ice cream stand, an excellent bakery, and a gourmet shop featuring local products *(see p82)*.

Bridge of Flowers, Shelburne Falls

Shelburne Falls, Massachusetts

Many artisans, musicians, and Sixties counterculture holdouts make their homes in this quirky village on the Mohawk Trail *(see p36)*. Cross the Deerfield River, which divides the town, on the Bridge of Flowers, a former railroad trestle heavily planted in blooms. The geological curiosity of glacial potholes scoured by a natural falls made the spot famous centuries ago. ◈ *Map C2*

Grafton, Vermont

This genteel village bunched around a 200-year-old tavern epitomizes rustic Vermont charm. Grafton Village Cheese Company makes top Vermont cheddars *(see p99)*.

Old Lyme, Connecticut

If Old Lyme was not actually the cradle of American Impressionism, it was at least the art movement's summer camp from 1899 into the 1930s. Surprisingly little of either the landscape or the town has changed since that artistic heyday. Unlock the history with a visit to the Florence Griswold House (see p92), where many of the artists lodged. 🗺 Map D5

Littleton, New Hampshire

In 1913, Littleton author Eleanor H. Porter created Pollyanna, the world's most optimistic character, and this Ammonoosuc River mill town at the edge of the White Mountains and New Hampshire's timber forests remains an upbeat place. Don't miss the world's longest candy counter at Chutter General Store (Main St.), or the Littleton Grist Mill (Mill St.). 🗺 Map L3

Watch Hill, Rhode Island

The giddy gingerbread architecture of Westerly's seaside village of Watch Hill betrays its Victorian roots – there's even a Victorian tea shop – but even sport fishermen come here for the perfect confluence of surf and shoreline currents (see p81).

New London, New Hampshire

Without the overhead power lines and asphalt on the roads, New London would look as if time had stopped around 1850. Home to Colby-Sawyer College, a prestigious liberal arts school, New London bustles during the summer as the shopping and dining center for Lake Sunapee vacationers; another draw is the Barn Playhouse's summer stock theater season. 🗺 Map L5

New London, park and bandstand

Kingfield, Maine

Gateway to the Sugarloaf USA ski resort (see p54), this characterful mountain village is a favorite with outdoors enthusiasts. The Stanley Museum chronicles the achievements of twin native sons Francis Edgar and Freelan Oscar Stanley, best known for inventing the steam-powered Stanley Steamer cars. Their sister Chansonetta's documentary photographs capture rural life. 🗺 Map N2
• Stanley Museum: 40 School St., Kingfield, ME; 207 265 2729; open year round; adm; www.stanleymuseum.org

Left **The village of Old Harbor, Block Island** Right **Cadillac Mountain, Mount Desert Island**

TOP 10 Islands

1 Monhegan Island, ME

Every seagull, twig, and moss-covered rock on Monhegan must have been painted over the century or so since this fishing outpost off mid-coast Maine became a summer art colony. Once the summer folk have gone, the fishermen return *(see p121)*.

Artist at work, Monhegan Island

2 Nantucket Island, MA

Thirty miles (48 km) off Cape Cod, Nantucket made its name through adventurous whaling and austere Quaker businessmen, who set the style with modest shingled homes. Pristine beaches, fascinating museums, and upscale shopping are among its present-day attractions. ✎ *Map H5 • Hyline Cruises: Ocean St. Dock, Hyannis; 508 778 2600; www.hy-linecruises.com*

3 Block Island, RI

Between Long Island and the Rhode Island coast, this tiny island looks like a tintype of a Victorian resort. Its beaches, nature reserves, and historic lighthouses are best explored on a bike *(see p82)*.

4 Isles of Shoals, NH

These nine unforested rocky islands stand so far offshore that they were first used by English, Basque, and Breton fishermen as camps to dry their catch in the summer sun. ✎ *Map N6 • Portsmouth Harbor Cruises, Ceres St. Dock; 603 436 8084; Jun–Sep: Tue–Fri; adm; www.portsmouthharbor.com*

5 Mount Desert Island, ME

This big island shaped like a baseball catcher's mitt is home to the unspoiled paradise of Acadia National Park and the summer resort town of Bar Harbor *(see pp10–11)*.

6 Thimble Islands, CT

Stories abound about the Thimble Islands, a cluster of diminutive islets located just off the Connecticut coast. On a narrated scenic cruise you'll likely hear a few of those tales, including the legend that pirate Captain Kidd buried treasure on Money Island. His gold hasn't been found – yet. ✎ *Map C6 • Thimble Island Cruise: Stony Creek; 203 488 8905; Jun–mid-Oct; www.thimbleislandcruise.com*

One of the many picturesque islets of the Thimbles

Note: the Isles of Shoals are privately owned, and visitors can make day trips only to Appledore, the site of a famous garden.

Martha's Vineyard, MA
Martha's Vineyard has something for every taste, from proper Edgartown and the gingerbread architecture of Oak Bluffs to the sacred multicolored clay cliffs of the Aquinnah Wampanoag tribe. ◈ *Map G5 • Steamship Authority: Woods Hole Terminal; 508 477 8600; www. islandferry.com*

Oak Bluffs, Martha's Vineyard

Isle au Haut, ME
With primeval quaking bogs along the forested park trails and wild, wave-pounded bluffs, this craggy rock a few miles from Stonington offers the attractions of Mount Desert Island without the crowds. ◈ *Map R4 • Isle au Haut Boat Services: Seabreeze Ave., Stonington; 207 367 5193; www.isleauhaut.com*

Boston Harbor Islands, MA
The Boston Harbor Islands have sandy hiking and nature trails, lifeguard-protected beaches, and even a few old forts to explore. Reach them by ferry from Boston's Long Wharf. ◈ *Map F3 • 617 223 8666 • May–Oct • www.bostonislands.org*

Burnt Island, ME
Cruise to this tiny island just outside Boothbay Harbor for a unique program illuminating the life of the lightkeeper and his family, who lived here circa 1950. ◈ *Map P4 • Balmy Days Cruises: Pier 8, Boothbay Harbor; 207 633 2284; 1:45pm Mon & Thu mid-Jul–early Sep; adm; www.balmydayscruises.com*

Top 10 Lighthouses

Sheffield Island
Handsome stone lighthouse built in 1868. ◈ *Norwalk Harbor, CT • Map B6*

Stonington Harbor
Granite lighthouse, now a museum. ◈ *7 Water St., Stonington, CT • Map E5*

West Quoddy Head
Iconic candy-striped light, 1857, marks easternmost point in US. ◈ *Quoddy Head State Park, Lubec, ME • Map R6*

Marshall Point
Offshore light connected by walkway to keeper's house, where there's a small museum. ◈ *Marshall Point Rd., Port Clyde, ME • Map Q4*

Pemaquid Point
Built high on dramatic ledges in 1835, Pemaquid Point remains an essential navigational aid. ◈ *Off Rte. 130, Bristol, ME • Map P4*

Portsmouth Harbor
Built in 1878, this is the latest of several on New Castle island since 1771. ◈ *off Rte. 1B, New Castle, NH • Map N6*

Beavertail
Third oldest light on the eastern seaboard (1783). ◈ *Beavertail State Park, Jamestown, RI • Map E5*

Highland
Highest light on New England mainland, atop bluff over Cape Cod National Seashore. ◈ *N. Truro, MA • Map H3*

Nobska Point
Visible for 16 miles (26 km) at sea, Nobska sits on the Shining Sea Bike Path. ◈ *Falmouth, MA • Map G5*

Great Point
Rebuilt in 1986 as a historic replica in Coskata-Coatue Wildlife Refuge. ◈ *Nantucket Island, MA • Map H5*

Left **Crane Beach with artist group** Right **The boardwalk, Hammonasset Beach State Park**

TOP 10 Ocean Beaches

1 Reid State Park, Georgetown, ME
Reid State Park beaches are long strands of brown sand backed by high dunes – the antithesis of the "rocky coast of Maine." Mile Beach and Half Mile Beach have lifeguards, changing rooms, and snack bars in summer. Swim safely along stretches sheltered from the ocean by sand bars, or break out the surf boards for more exposed parts of the beach. ◈ *Map P4 • Adm*

2 Crane Beach, Ipswich, MA
This 7-mile (11-km) stretch of copious white sand is one of New England's most picturesque swimming beaches. Pack binoculars; Crane is legendary for its diversity of bird species, although some nesting grounds may be off-limits between May and early August. ◈ *Map G2 • Adm*

3 Hammonasset Beach State Park, Madison, CT
More than 2 miles (3.2 km) of brown sand beaches lapped by the gentle waves of Long Island

Hampton Beach

Sound lure summer swimmers and sunbathers in droves, but Connecticut's longest shorefront park also boasts an excellent nature center at Meigs Point. Fishermen stake out positions here early for excellent bluefish and striped bass fishing. ◈ *Map C5 • Adm • Camping late May–mid-Oct*

4 Misquamicut State Beach, Westerly, RI
One of the most popular family beaches in New England, Misquamicut (miss-KWAHM-i-cut) packs intense summer entertainment into a relatively short stretch of white sand. Most rides, amusement stands, and food kiosks open only late June to August and some fall weekends, but the beach is accessible all year. Parking lots fill early on summer weekends. ◈ *Map E5 • Adm*

5 Hampton Beach, Hampton, NH
Small, decorous state beaches dot Hampton's shoreline, but the main village beach is easily the most raucous, with outdoor concerts, sandcastle competitions, a flurry of summer activities, and a strip of souvenir shops and casual eateries. In summer the town is bilingual, reflecting its popularity with Quebec vacationers. Swimming is good, but surf from offshore storms can make it challenging. ◈ *Map N6*

Admission to beaches is free unless otherwise stated, but parking fees may apply.

Ogunquit Beach, Ogunquit, ME

A 2-mile (3.2-km) cove lined with brown sand, Ogunquit Beach is well served by a summer trolley system that makes parking a cinch. The south end of the beach terminates at romantic Marginal Way, a clifftop walking path through thickets of roses to the shops, restaurants, and copious art galleries of Perkins Cove. ◈ Map N5

Surfers on Ogunquit Beach

Easton's Beach, Newport, RI

Surfers swarm the sands of Easton's, just below Newport's Cliff Walk, when the winds turn around from the northeast and waves crash along the eastern end. But even when the surf is up, the west end remains a terrific swimming beach for children – assuming you can tear them away from the historic carousel. Surfboard, beach chair, and bathhouse rentals available in summer. ◈ Map F5 • Adm

Old Orchard Beach, Old Orchard, ME

Old Orchard has been a razzle-dazzle resort beach since trains first ran here in 1842. Three miles (5 km) of main beach guarantee plenty of room for sunbathing, swimming, kite-flying, and sandcastle-building. Shops, amusements, and rides ensure no one ever gets bored. In summer there's also a lively bar scene (see p120).

Coast Guard Beach, Eastham, MA

Arguably the best swimming beach on Cape Cod, Coast Guard Beach marks the beginning of the 30-mile Great Beach of the Cape Cod National Seashore. A long and generous slope of sand leads down to the ocean, so the beach is never crowded. Stroll southward onto Nauset Spit to watch shore birds in summer, seals in winter. ◈ Map H4 • Adm

Old Silver Beach, Falmouth, MA

This beautiful beach overlooking Buzzards Bay has warm summer waters, low waves, and a very gradual drop-off, making it an ideal swimming spot for young kids. Half the beach is reserved for Falmouth residents; the other half is open to all. Facing west over the ocean, Old Silver has some of New England's most spec-tacular sunsets. ◈ Map G4 • Adm

Left **Worcester Art Museum** Center **"Moon Bed," Peabody Essex Museum** Right **Mass MoCA**

🔟 Art Museums

1 Museum of Fine Arts, Boston, MA

Highlights of this world-class art museum include major holdings of Asian, Egyptian, and Nubian art, and the most important Monet collection outside of Paris. ✪ *465 Huntington Ave. • Map S6 • 617 267 9300 • Open 10am–4:45pm Mon–Tue, Sat–Sun, 10am–9:45pm Wed–Fri • Adm • www.mfa.org*

Egyptian mummy, Museum of Fine Arts

2 Portland Museum of Art, Portland, ME

Visit Maine's largest art museum to see the work of American landscape painters such as Winslow Homer, Fitz Henry Lane, and Marsden Hartley. ✪ *7 Congress Sq. • Map N4 • 207 775 6148 • Open 10am–5pm Tue–Sun (to 9pm Fri); 10am–5pm Mon (end May–mid-Oct) • Adm • www.portlandmuseum.org*

3 Wadsworth Atheneum, Hartford, CT

America's oldest public art museum has New England's best collection of the startlingly oversized landscape canvases of the Hudson River School. ✪ *600 Main St. • Map C4 • 860 278 2670 • Open 11am–5pm Wed–Fri, 10am–5pm Sat–Sun • Adm • www.wadsworthatheneum.org*

4 Worcester Art Museum, MA

A fascinating collection of pre-Columbian art from Mexico and Central America, and some striking Roman mosaics are good reasons to visit this small general art museum. ✪ *55 Salisbury St. • Map E3 • 508 799 4406 • Open 11am–5pm Wed–Fri, Sun, 10am–5pm Sat • Adm • www.worcesterart.org*

5 Currier Museum of Art, Manchester, NH

In addition to its emphasis on 19th-century painting, the Currier Museum's collection embraces dynamic contemporary art as well. ✪ *150 Ash St. • Map M6 • 603 669 6144 • Open 11am–5pm Sun, Mon, Wed–Fri, 10am–5pm Sat • Adm • www.currier.org*

Central courtyard, Gardner Museum

6 Isabella Stewart Gardner Museum, Boston, MA

One of the all-time great private collectors, Gardner built a Renaissance-style palace to array her 2,500-object collection on three floors. ✪ *280 The Fenway • Map S6 • 617 566 1401 • Open 11am–5pm Tue–Sun • Adm • www.gardnermuseum.org*

 From Apr–mid-Jan, tour the Currier Museum's Zimmerman House to see architect Frank Lloyd Wright's radical "Usonian" style.

7 Peabody Essex Museum, Salem, MA

Staggering collections of China Trade treasures, historic furniture, and Asian art fill this soaring building by top architect Moshe Safdie. ⊗ *East India Sq.*
• *Map F2 • 978 745 9500 • Open 10am–5pm Tue–Sun • Adm • www.pem.org*

8 The Clark, Williamstown, MA

French Impressionists and English landscape artists are at the core of this diversified collection in a rural setting.
⊗ *225 South St. • Map B2 • 413 458 2303 • Open 10am–5pm Tue–Sun (daily in Jul & Aug) • Adm Jun–Oct; free Nov–May • www.clarkart.edu*

9 Mass MoCA, North Adams, MA

The museum focuses on new work by living artists, and also stages dance, avant-garde theater, and performance art.
⊗ *1040 Mass MoCA Way • Map B2 • 413 662 2111 • Open Jul–Sep: 10am–6pm daily; Oct–Jun: 11am–5pm Wed–Mon • Adm • www.massmoca.org*

Miniature circus parade, Shelburne Museum

10 Shelburne Museum, VT

From elaborately stitched quilts to two elaborate miniature circuses, the museum celebrates American folk art and ingenuity.
⊗ *Rte. 7, Shelburne • Map J3 • 802 985 3346 • Open mid-May–late Oct: 10am–5pm Mon–Sat, noon–5pm Sun • Adm • www.shelburnemuseum.org*

Top 10 Artists of New England

1 John Singleton Copley (1738–1815)
America's first great portraitist, Bostonian Copley fled to England during the Revolution.

2 Fitz Henry Lane (1805–65)
Largely self-tutored, Gloucester-based Lane revolutionized the handling of light in seascapes.

3 Winslow Homer (1836–1910)
Homer is most celebrated for his vigorous Maine seascapes.

4 Childe Hassam (1859–1935)
Hassam painted the streets of Boston and the Connecticut landscape with equal flourish.

5 Marsden Hartley (1877–1943)
Hartley painted powerful abstract landscapes of his native Maine.

6 Edward Hopper (1882–1967)
Summering on the coast, Hopper painted scenes full of psychological nuance.

7 Rockwell Kent (1882–1971)
Painter and illustrator Kent is best known for his stark Arctic landscapes.

8 Norman Rockwell (1894–1978)
Rockwell championed home-spun American values in covers for *The Saturday Evening Post*.

9 Louise Nevelson (1899–1988)
Raised in Maine, Nevelson is known for her Abstract Expressionist sculptural assemblages.

10 Andrew Wyeth (1917–2009)
Wyeth is noted for the almost photographic realism of his *tempera* landscapes.

The Shelburne has some outdoor exhibits, including a lighthouse, an 1890 train station, and a 220-ft (67-m) steamship.

Left **RISD Museum of Art** Center **Hood Museum of Art** Right **Smith College Museum of Art**

🔟 University Museums

1 Yale University Art Museums, New Haven, CT

The largest collection of British art outside the UK is kept at the Yale Center for British Art, designed by modernist architect Louis B. Kahn (1901–74). The Yale University Art Gallery, an earlier Kahn building of 1953, is noted for its American paintings and decorative arts. ✪ *Map C5 • Yale Center for British Art: 1080 Chapel St.; 203 432 2800; open 10am–5pm Tue–Sat, noon–5pm Sun; free; www.ycba.yale.edu • Yale University Art Gallery: 1111 Chapel St.; 203 432 0600; open 10am–5pm Tue–Sat, 1–6pm Sun; free; www.artgallery.yale.edu*

2 RISD Museum of Art, Providence, RI

Students at New England's premier art and design school seek inspiration here. The historically encyclopedic collection of more than 84,000 objects is notable for late-19th-century painting (including French Impressionism), as well as post-1960 arts in various media. Contemporary studio crafts and furniture are also strong. Early American furniture stars in the decorative arts wing. ✪ *224 Benefit St. • Map E4 • 401 454 6500 • Open 10am–5pm Tue–Sun • Adm • www.risdmuseum.org*

3 Harvard Art Museum, Cambridge, MA

One of the world's most wide-ranging university art museums, it boasts outstanding collections of ancient Greek, medieval, Renaissance, Impressionist, Expressionist, and Asian art. ✪ *485 Broadway • Map F2 • 617 495 9400 • Open 10am–5pm Tue–Sat, 1–5pm Sun • Adm • www.harvardartmuseums.org*

4 Smith College Museum of Art, Northampton, MA

Since its 19th-century founding, Smith has collected contemporary art. Rufino Tamayo's *Nature and the Artist: The Work of Art and the Observer*, commissioned by the college in 1943, offers a rare chance to see a work by one of Mexico's leading muralists. ✪ *Elm St. • Map C3 • 413 585 2760 • Open 10am–4pm Tue–Sat, noon–4pm Sun • Adm • http://scma.smith.edu/artmuseum*

5 Williams College Museum of Art, Williamstown, MA

With its emphasis on modern art, this museum is the perfect complement to the Old Masters and Impressionists at the neighboring Clark *(see p45)*. Don't miss *Morning in a City*, by American realist Edward Hopper (1882–1967). ✪ *15 Lawrence Hall Dr. • Map B2 • 413 597 2429 • Open 10am–5pm Tue–Sat, 1–5pm Sun • Free • www.wcma.org*

Williams College Museum of Art

Renovation is ongoing at Harvard Art Museum till 2013. Meanwhile, a selection of exhibits is housed at the Sackler Museum.

Peary-MacMillan Arctic Museum

Peary-MacMillan Arctic Museum, Brunswick, ME

Named for Bowdoin College alumni Robert E. Peary (1856–1920) and Donald B. MacMillan (1874–1970), this museum brings their daring Arctic explorations to life. Natural history specimens, Inuit artifacts, and photographs offer insight on the cultures of the far north. ⬥ Hubbard Hall, Bowdoin College • Map P4 • 207 725 3416 • Open 10am–5pm Tue–Sat, 2–5pm Sun • Free • www.bowdoin.edu/arctic-museum

Hood Museum of Art, Hanover, NH

Assyrian stone reliefs from the palace of Ashurnasirpal (around 900 BC) are the Hood's prize display. Strong selections of Native American, Melanesian, and sub-Saharan art bring a global sweep to the galleries. ⬥ Dartmouth College • Map L4 • 603 646 2808 • Open 10am–5pm Tue, Thu–Sat, 10am–9pm Wed, noon–5pm Sun • Free • www.hoodmuseum.dartmouth.edu

Ballard Institute and Museum of Puppetry, Storrs, CT

The key exhibits at this unique museum are the puppets of Frank Ballard (1929–2010), a drama professor who set up America's first degree course in puppetry. ⬥ Depot Campus, 6 Bourne Pl., University of Connecticut • Map D4 • 860 486 0339 • Open noon–5pm Fri–Sun late Apr–late Nov • Donation • www.bimp.uconn.edu

Harvard Museum of Natural History, Cambridge, MA

As the public face of three Harvard research institutions, this museum combines the charm of old-fashioned artifacts with the thrill of cutting-edge science. The Glass Flowers are famous worldwide for their utterly realistic re-creation of plants and blossoms. Dinosaur skeletons, gemstones and meteorites invariably elicit awe. ⬥ 26 Oxford St. • Map F2 • 617 495 3045 • Open 9am–5pm daily • Adm • www.hmnh.harvard.edu

Culinary Arts Museum at Johnson and Wales University, Providence, RI

This small museum of the culinary arts and hospitality industry never fails to delight, with its historic roadside diners, a fascinating collection of kitchen gadgets, and even a rundown on state and presidential dinners. See how the hierarchy of the professional kitchen developed, and learn about great chefs through the ages. ⬥ 315 Harborside Blvd. • Map E4 • 401 598 2805 • Open 10am–5pm Tue–Sun • Adm • www.culinary.org

Left **Ben and Jerry's** Center **Boston Children's Museum** Right **Roger Williams Park and Zoo**

Children's Attractions

1 Boston Children's Museum

This pioneer in hands-on learning fills two former wool warehouses on the Boston waterfront. Children can scale a three-story climbing sculpture, explore the magic of soap bubbles, or join in short plays and shows on KidStage. *300 Congress St. • Map X4 • 617 426 6500 • Open 10am–5pm Sat–Thu, 10am–9pm Fri • Adm • www.bostonkids.org*

2 Dinosaur State Park, Rocky Hill, CT

Children are awestruck by more than 500 dinosaur tracks preserved beneath a geodesic dome. Life-size dioramas re-create scenes from the Jurassic and Triassic eras. *400 West St. • Map C4 • 860 529 8423 • Open 9am–4:30pm daily (exhibit center Tue–Sun only) • Adm • www.dinosaurstatepark.org*

Ancient tracks, Dinosaur State Park

3 Roger Williams Park and Zoo, Providence, RI

You can ride the carousel or take a boat ride on the lake in this sprawling park, but save time for the zoo – one of the country's best, with naturalistic settings. *1000 Elmwood Ave. • Map E4 • 401 785 3510 • Open 9am–4pm daily • Adm • www.rwpzoo.org*

4 New England Aquarium, Boston

Kids will love the acrobatics of the harbor seals, the antics of more than 80 penguins, and the shark and ray tank. *Central Wharf • Map X3 • 617 973 5200 • Open Jul–Aug: 9am–6pm Sun–Thu, 9am–7pm Fri–Sat; Sep–Jun: 9am–5pm Mon–Fri, 9am–6pm Sat–Sun • Adm • www.neaq.org*

5 McAuliffe-Shepard Discovery Center, Concord, NH

Kids are encouraged to reach for the stars at this space exploration center named for astronauts Alan B. Shepard and Christa McAuliffe. *2 Institute Dr. • Map M5 • 603 271 7827 • Open 10am–5pm Mon–Thu, Sat & Sun, 10am–9pm Fri • Adm • www.starhop.com*

6 Six Flags New England, Agawam, MA

Some of the fastest, tallest, wildest, and most gut-wrenching thrill rides in the country await at this amusement park by the Connecticut River. *Rte. 159 • Map C3 • 413 786 9300 • Open Apr–Oct, call for hours • Adm • www.sixflags.com*

Basketball Hall of Fame

 Note: the New England Aquarium also operates summertime whale-watch excursions with marine naturalists.

7 Basketball Hall of Fame, Springfield, MA

This complex in the birthplace of basketball celebrates the sport with footage of games, star players' memorabilia, and interactive exhibits for the kids.
§ 1000 W. Columbus Ave. • Map C3
• 413 781 6500 or 877 4HOOPLA
• Open 10am–4pm Tue–Fri, Sun, 10am–5pm Sat • Adm • www.hoophall.com

8 Lake Compounce, Bristol, CT

A 1911 carousel, a 1927 roller coaster, and an antique trolley maintain the feel of an old-fashioned amusement park.
§ 186 Enterprise Dr. • Map C4 • 860 583 3300 • Open May–Oct, call for schedule
• Adm • www.lakecompounce.com

9 Mystic Aquarium, CT

The 70 exhibits of this striking aquarium display 12,000 fishes, invertebrates, and marine mammals from more than 425 species. § 55 Coogan Blvd. • Map D5 • 860 572 5955
• Open daily, Apr–Oct: 9am–5pm; Mar & Nov: 9am–4pm; Dec–Feb: 10am–4pm
• Adm • www.mysticaquarium.org

Beluga whale, Mystic Aquarium

10 Ben & Jerry's Ice Cream Factory, Waterbury, VT

Ben Cohen and Jerry Greenfield never thought business should be dull, and the factory tour of Ben & Jerry's is a real hoot. The goal, of course, is the tasting room at the end, where you might even sample new flavors in development (see p103).

Top 10 Carousels

1 Flying Horse Carousel
Beachfront Dare carousel is one of New England's oldest. § Bay St., Watch Hill, RI • Map E5 • 401 348 6007 • Adm

2 Fall River Carousel
Built by the Philadelphia Toboggan Co. in 1920.
§ Battleship Cove, Fall River, MA • Map F4 • 508 678 1100 • Adm

3 Shelburne Museum
Vintage 1920s carousel operates outside the museum's Circus Building (see pp45).

4 Crescent Park Carousel
Charles I.D. Looff showcase. § 700 Bullocks Point Ave., East Providence, RI • Map F4 • 401 435 7518 • Adm

5 Bushnell Park Carousel
Three-row hand-carved wooden carousel. § Bushnell Park, Hartford, CT • Map C4 • 860 232 6710 • Adm

6 Flying Horses Carousel
1876–8 Dare Co. model. § Oak Bluffs Ave., Oak Bluffs, Martha's Vineyard, MA • Map G5 • 508 693 9481 • Adm

7 Slater Memorial Park
1895 carousel includes a camel, a giraffe, a lion, and two chariots. § Pawtucket, RI • Map E4 • 401 728 0500 ext.252 • Adm

8 Story Land
Unusual early-20th-century German carousel. § Rte. 16, Glen, NH • Map M4 • 603 383 4186 • Adm

9 Heritage State Park
1929 carousel with 20 standing horses, 28 jumpers.
§ 221 Appleton St., Holyoke, MA • Map C3 • 413 538 9838 • Adm

10 Lighthouse Point Park
1916 carousel with 72 original figures. § 2 Lighthouse Point Rd., New Haven, CT • Map C5 • 203 946 8327 • Adm

Left **Gropius House** Center *Turkey Pond,* **Andrew Wyeth** Right **Orchard House**

Personal Museums

1 Mark Twain House, Hartford, CT

Tiffany interiors feature in the home of the great storyteller. The adjoining museum revolves around Twain (1835–1910) and his contemporaries.

Entrance, Mark Twain House

⬡ 351 Farmington Ave.
• Map C4 • 860 247 0998
• Open 9:30am–5:30pm Mon–Sat, noon–5:30pm Sun (Jan–Mar: closed Tue) • Adm • www.marktwainhouse.org

2 Orchard House, Concord, MA

Louisa May Alcott (1832–88) didn't just set her classic *Little Women* in Orchard House, she wrote it here, in 1868. ⬡ 399 Lexington Rd.
• Map F2 • 978 369 4118 • Open Apr–Oct: 10am–4:30pm Mon–Sat, 1–4:30pm Sun; Nov–Mar: 11am–3pm Mon–Fri, 10am–4:30pm Sat, 1–4:30pm Sun • Adm
• www.louisamayalcott.org

3 Longfellow House–Washington's Headquarters National Historic Site, Cambridge, MA

A visit to the home of poet Henry Wadsworth Longfellow (1807–82), one of America's most influential literary figures, lays bare both his

Henry Wadsworth Longfellow's home

triumphs and his tragedies, like the fire that killed his wife and so scarred his face that he grew his signature beard. ⬡ 105 Brattle St. • Map F2 • 617 876 4491 • Open Jun–Oct: 10am–4:30pm Wed–Sun • www.nps.gov/long

4 The Mount, Lenox, MA

This Berkshires estate dating from 1902 showcases the design and decorating sensibilities of literary giant Edith Wharton.
⬡ 2 Plunkett St. • Map B3 • 413 551 5111
• Open early May–Oct: 10am–5pm daily
• Adm • www.edithwharton.org

5 Saint-Gaudens National Historic Site, Cornish, NH

A house museum evoking the rustic idyll of the art colony that grew up around Augustus Saint-Gaudens (1848–1907), America's leading sculptor of the Beaux-Arts generation. ⬡ Rte. 12A • Map L5 • 603 675 2175 • Open late May–Oct: 9am–4:30pm daily; grounds open all year
• Adm • www.nps.gov/saga

6 Emily Dickinson Museum, Amherst, MA

The richly imaginative vision of poet Emily Dickinson (1830–86) flourished in this highly reclusive world – she rarely left her family home, except to visit her brother next door. ⬡ 280 Main St. • Map C2
• 413 542 8161 • Open Mar–Dec: 11am–4pm Wed–Sun; Jun–Aug: 10am–5pm •
Adm • www.emilydickinsonmuseum.org

7 Chesterwood, Stockbridge, MA

The home and studio of Daniel Chester French (1850–1931) vividly recalls the sculptor best known for his seated Abraham Lincoln in Washington, D.C.'s Lincoln Memorial. ⊗ 4 Williamsville Rd. • Map B3 • 413 298 3579 • Open late May–Oct: 10am–5pm daily • Adm • www.chesterwood.org

8 John F. Kennedy Presidential Library & Museum, Boston, MA

This museum chronicles JFK's 1,000 days in office, and touches on the man behind the myth. ⊗ Columbia Point • Map F3 • 617 514 1600 • Open 9am–5pm daily • Adm • www.jfklibrary.org

John F. Kennedy Library and Museum

9 Gropius House, Lincoln, MA

Explore the family home of the highly influential architect Walter Gropius (1883–1969). ⊗ 68 Baker Bridge Rd. • Map F2 • 781 259 8098 • Open 11am–4pm Wed–Sun (mid-Oct–May: Sat–Sun only) • Adm • www. historicnewengland.org

10 Farnsworth Art Museum, Rockland, ME

The art dynasty of N. C. Wyeth (1882–1945), Andrew Wyeth (1917–2009), and James Wyeth (b.1946) is celebrated here. ⊗ 16 Museum St. • Map Q3 • 207 596 6457 • Open 10am–5pm daily (Nov–late May: Wed–Sun) • Adm • www.farnsworthmuseum.org

Top 10 New England Books

1 Walden by Henry David Thoreau
Philosophical musings in the Massachusetts woods remain a key text in American thought.

2 Country of the Pointed Firs by Sarah Orne Jewett
Revolutionary psychological novel about women in rural coastal Maine, c.1900.

3 Outermost House by Henry Beston
Account of a year living on Cape Cod's Great Beach.

4 New Hampshire by Robert Frost
Pulitzer Prize-winning poetry collection contains much of Frost's most quoted verse.

5 Hotel New Hampshire by John Irving
Comic turns abound in literary novel of despair and redemption at an old resort hotel.

6 Mystic River by Dennis Lehane
Noir fiction reveals seamy undercurrents of life on the edge in South Boston.

7 Little Women by Louise May Alcott
The four March girls struggle to overcome character flaws.

8 Charlotte's Web by E. B. White
Children's classic fiction finds philosophy in the barnyard.

9 Witches of Eastwick by John Updike
Women of fictional Rhode Island town dabble in the occult in this parable of love and power.

10 Mortal Friends by James Carroll
The tale of Colman Brady, part Irish revolutionary, part Boston mobster.

Left **Mount Mansfield** Center **Mad River Glen** Right **Skiing in Sunday River**

TOP 10 Ski Mountains

1 Sunday River, Newry, ME
The most accessible of Maine's high-mountain skiing, Sunday River splashes across eight interconnected peaks, with 131 diverse trails served by 16 lifts (including four high-speed quads). Lights extend evening skiing on most weekends and holidays. Snowmaking on 92 per cent of terrain guarantees a long season. Evenings are enlived by the popular Shipyard Brew Haus microbrewery. Summer golf resort. ⚡ *15 South Ridge Rd. • Map M3 • 207 824 3000 • Ski: mid-Nov–mid-Apr • Adm • www.sundayriver.com*

2 Sugarloaf USA, Carrabasset Valley, ME
Sugarloaf caters to adventure skiers. Offering the only lift-served skiing above the treeline in the East, its 54 miles (87 km) of trails crisscross the second highest peak in Maine at 4,237 ft (1,291 m). The continuous vertical drop of 2,820 ft (860 m) is New England's longest. Fifty of Sugarloaf's 146 trails are rated either difficult (black diamond) or expert (double black diamond). Summer golf resort. ⚡ *5092 Sugarloaf Access Rd. • Map N2 • 207 237 2000 • Ski: mid-Nov–late Apr • Adm • www.sugarloaf.com*

3 Saddleback Mountain, Rangeley, ME
Remote but affordable wilderness skiing is the lure of Saddleback, which sprawls across a cluster of high alpine peaks covered with snow-frosted evergreens. Lifts bring skiers to elevations greater than 4,000 ft (1,219 m) for more than 2,000 vertical ft (609 m) of skiing. Less developed than many ski areas, Saddleback's summer activities lean toward guided mountain hiking and guided flyfishing. ⚡ *976 Saddleback Rd. • Map N2 • 207 864 5671 • Ski: Dec–Mar • Adm • www.saddlebackmaine.com*

4 Mount Mansfield, Stowe, VT
As the tallest of the Green Mountains, Mansfield challenges hikers every summer and fall. Come winter, Stowe Mountain Resort takes over the slopes with 116 trails and more mile-long lifts than any other resort in the East. With average annual snowfall of 333 inches (8.46m), Stowe has a long season of deep snow. Summer golf resort. ⚡ *5781 Mountain Rd. • Map K3 • 802 253 3000 • Ski: mid-Nov–mid-Apr • Adm • www.stowe.com*

Killington Peak

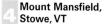

Killington, VT

Killington Resort stretches across six mountain areas in central Vermont, providing 140 ski trails. As New England's largest ski resort, it also features 20 lifts, including two express gondolas and five express chairs, that give access to the highest lift-served ski terrain in Vermont. For boarders there's The Stash and Dream Maker terrain parks and the 500-ft (152-m) Superpipe. ◈ 4763 Killington Rd. • Map K5 • 802 422 6200 • Ski: mid-Nov–mid-Apr • Adm • www.killington.com

Smugglers' Notch, Jeffersonville, VT

Smugglers' is an all-season family resort well known for its learn-to-ski programs and activities for kids. The resort stretches across three peaks, with 8 lifts serving 78 trails. Smugglers' skiing can be challenging, despite its family orientation; the Black Hole is the only triple black diamond trail in the Eastern US. Summer golf resort. ◈ 4323 Rte. 108 S. • Map K3 • 802 644 8851 • Ski: mid-Nov–mid-Apr • Adm • www.smuggs.com

Jay Peak, Jay, VT

Snuggled up against the Canadian border in northern Vermont, Jay Peak's glade skiing is ranked by experts as among the best in the US. Annual snowfall of 355 inches (9 m) reduces the need for snowmaking. The eight lifts serving 76 trails include a 60-passenger tramway. Summer golf resort. ◈ 4850 Rte. 242 • Map K2 • 802 988 2611 • Ski: Nov–early May • Adm • www.jaypeakresort.com

Mad River Glen, Waitsfield, VT

This mountain with some of the East's most challenging terrain is run by a co-op of hardcore skiers who keep it simple: no snowboards; a single-chair lift from 1948 that limits numbers on the slopes; and no fancy base lodge or hotels with hot tubs. ◈ Map K3 • 802 496 3551 • Ski: mid-Dec–early Apr • Adm • www.madriverglen.com

Attitash, Bartlett, NH

Not as big or challenging as some New England areas, Attitash (and attached Bear Peak) have vistas of the White Mountains to make the skiing memorable. The longest vertical drop is 1,750 ft (534 m), but 11 lifts serve 70 trails. ◈ Rte. 302 • Map M4 • 800 223 7669 • Ski: late Nov–Apr • Adm • www.attitash.com

Cannon Mountain, Franconia, NH

One of the oldest ski areas in the US, Cannon has a refreshingly noncommercial feel about it – not to mention spectacular White Mountains vistas from its 72 trails. ◈ 9 Franconia Notch State Park • Map L3 • 603 823 8800 • Ski: Nov–mid-Apr • Adm • www.cannonmt.com

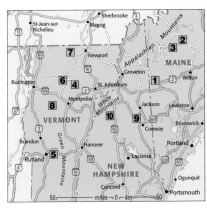

Left **Whale-watch cruises** Center **Hiking** Right **Fishing**

Other Outdoor Activities and Sports

1 Whale-Watch Cruises

Large pods of several whale species summer on Stellwagen Bank off the Massachusetts coast. Take a cruise from Gloucester or Provincetown to look for finback, minke, and humpback whales, as well as dolphins and other smaller toothed whales. ✆ *7 Seas: 63 Rogers St., Gloucester, MA; Map G2; 888 283 1776; open late Apr–Oct; adm; www.7seas-whalewatch.com • Dolphin Fleet: MacMillan Wharf, Provincetown, MA; Map H3; 508 240 3636; open mid-Apr–Oct; adm; www.whalewatch.com*

2 Schooner Sails

Seals, seabirds, porpoises, and whales become your neighbors as you sail where the winds take you with the schooners of Maine's windjammer fleet. ✆ *Rockland and Camden, ME • Map Q3 • 800 807 WIND (9463) • Open Jun–Sep • Adm • www.sailmainecoast.com*

3 White-Water Rafting

White-water rafting is hugely popular in Maine. Many trips depart from The Forks, a hamlet on the Kennebec. ✆ *West Forks, ME • Map P1 • 800 723 8633 • Open May–early Oct • Adm • www.raftmaine.com*

White-water rafting

4 Cross-Country Skiing

North-central Vermont is the epicenter of cross-country skiing. The Trapp family (of *Sound of Music* fame) introduced Nordic skiing in Stowe. Craftsbury Nordic Center is home to legendary cross-country ski races. ✆ *Trapp Family Lodge: 700 Trapp Hill Rd., Stowe, VT; Map K3; 802 253 8511; www.trapp family.com • Craftsbury Nordic Center: 535 Lost Nation Rd., Craftsbury Common, VT; Map K2; 802 586 7767; open mid-Dec–Mar; adm; www.craftsbury.com*

5 Bird-Watching

Observe shore birds, as well as warblers and other migratory species, at Wellfleet Bay Wildlife Sanctuary on Cape Cod. The Audubon Society in Greenwich, Connecticut, runs a convivial annual count. ✆ *Wellfleet Bay: Rte. 6, Wellfleet, MA; Map H4; 508 349 2615; trails open 8am–dusk daily; adm; www.massaudubon.org • Audubon: 613 Riversville Rd., Greenwich, CT; Map A6; 203 869 5272; open 9am–5pm daily; adm; http://greenwich.audubon.org*

6 Bicycling

Some of New England's best bike routes follow old rail lines. In Massachusetts, Minuteman Rail Trail cuts from Cambridge through Lexington and Concord. East Bay Bike Path is a scenic tour of Narragansett Bay from Providence, Rhode Island. The Ashuelot Rail Trail from Keene to Hinsdale, New Hampshire, is a great way to explore covered bridges. ✆ *www.traillink.com*

Hiking

7 Two premier US long-distance hiking trails cross New England. The Appalachian Trail begins in Georgia, crossing Vermont and New Hampshire before ending in Maine. The Long Trail traverses Vermont from south to north.

🔗 *Appalachian Trail: www.outdoors.org*
• *Long Trail: www.greenmountainclub.org*

Golf

8 Championship-level courses in New England include Samoset and Ocean Edge. 🔗 *Samoset: 220 Warrenton St., Rockport, ME; Map Q3; 207 594 2511; open May–Nov; adm; www.samosetresort.com • Ocean Edge: 2907 Main St., Brewster, MA; Map H4; 508 896 9000; open Apr–Nov; adm; www.oceanedge.com*

Kayaking and Canoeing

9 Paddle among the wading birds of Nauset Marsh, or through the pristine landscape of Maine's Allagash Wilderness. 🔗 *Nauset: Goose Hummock Shops, Rte. 6A, Orleans, MA; Map H4; 508 255 2620; open May–Oct; adm; www.goose.com • Allagash: Adventures in Maine, 273 East Rd., Fayette, ME; Map P3; 207 458 1573; open Jun–Sep; adm; www.adventuresinmaineguide.com*

Kayaking on the Kennebec River

Fishing

10 Orvis runs fly-fishing courses in Manchester, Vermont. Frances Fleet, of Galilee, Rhode Island offers deep-sea trips. 🔗 *Orvis: 4180 Main St., Manchester, VT; Map K6; 866 531 6213; www.orvis.com • Frances Fleet: 33 State St., Narragansett, RI; Map E5; 401 783 4988; open all year (saltwater); Apr–Sep (fresh); adm; www.francesfleet.com*

Top 10 Spectator Sports

1 Boston Red Sox
Baseball's most hallowed park. 🔗 *Fenway Park, Boston, MA • Map S5 • Apr–Oct*

2 New England Patriots
The Patriots are perennial Super Bowl contenders. 🔗 *Gillette Stadium, Foxborough, MA • Map F3 • Sep–Jan*

3 Boston Celtics
Hoop dreams ramp up each fall as the Celtics take the court. 🔗 *TD Garden, Boston, MA • Map F2 • Oct–May*

4 Boston Bruins
One of the founding teams of the National Hockey League. 🔗 *TD Garden, Boston, MA • Map F2 • Oct–Apr*

5 Head of the Charles Regatta
The world's largest two-day rowing event, on the Charles River between Cambridge and Boston. 🔗 *Map F2 • Mid–Oct*

6 Boston Marathon
The world's oldest annual marathon, from Hopkinton to Boston. 🔗 *Map F2 • Apr*

7 New Hampshire Motor Speedway
Sports cars, stock cars, and even go-karts thrill fans with their speed. 🔗 *Loudon, NH • Map M5 • Apr–Oct*

8 Newport Regatta
Topsail racing in the home of American yachting (see p15).

9 US National Toboggan Championships
Open-entry field of contestants at the Camden Snow Bowl. 🔗 *Camden, ME • Map Q3 • Feb*

10 Stowe Derby
Race from Mt. Mansfield to Stowe village on one pair of skis tests combined alpine and Nordic skills. 🔗 *Stowe, VT • Map K3 • late Feb*

 Note: if you're planning to kayak or canoe in Nauset or Allagash, Nauset is a day trip; Allagash excursions usually run 5–7 days.

57

Left **New England lobsters** Centre **Rhode Island clams** Right **Jonnycakes with egg and bacon**

New England Foods

1 Lobster

One of the pleasures of New England summer is setting a steamed lobster on a picnic table, cracking it with a rock, and savoring the sweet meat with melted butter. *Homarus americanus*, often called "Maine lobster," is the world's largest crustacean, and is generally served at weights of 1¼–3 lb (0.56–1.36 kg).

2 Clams

It's easy to get confused by New England clams. "Quahog" is the Native-American name for the hard-shelled clam *Mercenaria mercenaria*, but the bivalve has other aliases. Small ones, known as "littlenecks," are served as the ever-popular battered-and-fried clam. Medium-sized quahogs are called "cherrystones," and are often eaten raw. Big ones are stuffed and baked.

3 Oysters

New England oysters are found on sandy bottoms all along the coast, but those cultured in beds near Damariscotta, Maine; Wellfleet, Massachusetts; and Norwalk, Connecticut are celebrated for their delicate, distinctive flavors.

4 Maple Syrup

Nothing tames a Yankee sour-puss like pouring on the maple syrup over a stack of pancakes or waffles. In late winter, you might

Giant scallops with bacon and succotash

encounter sugar houses in the north of New England boiling down the sap of sugar maple trees. Stop for a jug – you'll never find it cheaper.

5 Scallops

Scallops were popular in New England cooking long before they became a mainstay of gourmet restaurants. Look for them sautéed in butter, breaded and deep-fried, or tossed with linguine, herbs, and olive oil. Scallops are on almost every menu, not least because New Bedford, Massachusetts, lands more scallops than any other port in the world.

Sakonnet oysters in half-shell

6 Cheese

You'll find world-class farmstead cheeses all across New England. Small dairies make everything from fresh goat's milk chevre to aged, pungent blues. Somewhat larger Vermont cheese companies also produce superb American cheddar and Colby cheeses.

The tart bog cranberry was widely used by Native Americans. It has been cultivated on Cape Cod since 1816.

7 Blueberries

Whether you prefer the light blueberry accent of a muffin or the supreme intensity of a blueberry pie, there's no substitute for the tiny "wild" lowbush blueberry. Most wild blueberries are harvested in Maine from late July through August, but they freeze well, so blueberry baked treats are available all year.

8 Cranberries

Popular in juices and muffins, cranberries are best known for the sugary sauce served as part of traditional Thanksgiving dinner. Massachusetts still produces about half the US crop.

Cranberries

9 Stone-ground Cornmeal

Order a jonnycake – a sweet cornmeal pancake cooked on a griddle – at any Rhode Island diner, and you're enjoying a culinary tradition that goes back to the region's first European colonists and the Native Americans before them.

10 Heirloom Apples

Keep your eyes peeled for orchard farmstands selling apples in the fall. Many historic apple varieties can be traced to their New England birthplace by name (Roxbury Russet, Westfield-Seek-No-Further). Preservation efforts launched in the 1980s have born fruit in the widespread availability of several dozen historic apples.

Top 10 Drinks

1 Moxie

Invented in 1876 by Augustin Thompson, a medical doctor, this soft drink with an appropriately medicinal aftertaste is the state beverage of Maine.

2 Apple Cider

Freshly pressed and unfiltered apple juice is widely available in the fall.

3 Sam Adams Lager

The flagship brew of the Boston Beer Company launched the national microbrewery revolution.

4 Del's Lemonade

The sole ingredients of this thirst-quenching Rhode Island favorite are lemon juice, sugar, and shaved ice.

5 Poland Spring Water

This brand of bottled water originating in a former Maine spa town is distributed widely in New England.

6 Coffee Milk

Rhode Island's official state drink is created by stirring coffee syrup into milk.

7 Sparkling Wines from Westport Rivers Winery

Estate-grown pinot noir and chardonnay grapes make New England's best bubbly.

8 Green Mountain Coffee

Gourmet coffee roaster's blends are sold throughout the region.

9 Sakonnet Vineyards Vidal Blanc

The signature wine of this small Rhode Island winery is crisp and dry with apricot and white peach nose.

10 Frappe

Pronounced "frap," this New England thick milkshake includes ice cream and syrup.

Rhode Island cornmeal is famed for its flavor and consistency.

Left **Clio** Center **Primo** Right **Al Forno**

🔟 Restaurants

1 Clio, Boston, MA
Chef-owner Ken Orringer is a national culinary star, whose sumptuous, creative American cuisine borrows freely from around the globe. Dishes range from sautéed salmon with grapefruit, kohlrabi, and licorice root to impeccable sushi and sashimi. A Boston "must-eat" (see p75).

Arrows

2 Arrows, Ogunquit, ME
Maine's most ostentatious restaurant serves spectacular salads from the organic kitchen garden along with inventive New American preparations of locally grown meats and sustainable fish. The 18th-century farmhouse setting adds a touch of rustic charm (see p123).

3 Brasserie Pip, Ivoryton, CT
Seasonal local ingredients feature prominently at this casual brasserie in the stylish Copper Beach Inn. Dishes range from steak-frites to a bouillabaisse of local fish. The oyster bar is one of the area's best (see p94).

4 Ristorante Massimo, Portsmouth, NH
New England seafood acquires an Italian accent here, in this sophisticated room in a historic waterfront building. Don't miss the yellowfin tuna and lobster with lemon risotto (see p115).

5 Chillingsworth, Brewster, MA
Even after a day on a Cape Cod beach, you can still indulge in exquisite French cuisine. An ever-changing multi-course meal is served in the historic dining rooms of a 300-year-old house. Light eaters may appreciate the more casual bistro, an airy café with an à la carte menu where it's fine to order just an appetizer and a dessert (see p77).

6 Restaurant at the Inn, Shelburne Farms, VT
Inn guests always admire the Shelburne Farms market garden, and the food tastes as good as it looks. Produce direct from this and other local farms goes into a seasonal menu of classic Continental dishes with an American accent. Meals are served in the elegant marble dining room, or on the outdoor terrace (see p105).

Inn at Shelburne Farms

 Recommend your favorite restaurant on **traveldk.com**

7 Primo Restaurant, Rockland, ME

Freshness is key at this coastal restaurant. The innovative menu depends on produce just pulled from the ground as well as local fish just pulled from the sea. The chef-owner raises her own produce and makes sausage from her own pigs (see p123).

8 Al Forno, Providence, RI

A wood-fired oven provides the searing heat essential for spectacular Northern Italian meat dishes like chorizo-stuffed quails with plum jam, as well as Al Forno's signature baked pasta dishes. The style is Italian; most ingredients are local (see p85).

Union League Café

9 Union League Café, New Haven, CT

New England meat, produce, and spectacular fish get the French brasserie treatment at this classy but cozy dining spot at the edge of Yale University. There's also an outstanding raw bar of New England shellfish (see p94).

10 Wheatleigh Hotel, Lenox, MA

The hotel may resemble a French chateau, but the elegant menu recalls fine dining at an English country house. High-season summer menus may include delights such as duck with chanterelles or diver scallop with parsnip and truffle (see p77).

Top 10 Places to Eat Seafood

1 Five Islands Lobster Co.
Georgetown pier lobster shack. Stunning views. ◎ 1447 Five Islands Rd., Georgetown, ME • Map P4 • 207 371 2990

2 Woodman's of Essex
Their fried clams are among the best. ◎ 121 Main St., Essex, MA • Map G2 • 978 768 6057

3 Evelyn's Drive-In
Famous for their stuffed clams. ◎ 2335 Main Rd., Tiverton, RI • Map F4 • 401 624 3100

4 Barking Crab
Clam-shack ambience comes to the Boston waterfront. ◎ 88 Sleeper St., Boston, MA • Map X4 • 617 426 CRAB

5 Abbott's Lobster in the Rough
Butter-drenched lobster meat in a bun – heavenly. ◎ 117 Pearl St., Noank, CT • Map D5 • 860 536 7719

6 Shaw's Fish & Lobster Wharf
Diners can watch lobster boats come and go in the narrow inlet. ◎ Rte. 32, New Harbor, ME • Map P4 • 207 677 2200

7 George's of Galilee
George's has had pick of the catch since 1948. ◎ 250 Sand Hill Cove Rd., Galilee, RI • Map E5 • 401 783 2306

8 Net Result
The menu varies with the catch; perfect fish. ◎ 79 Beach Rd., Vineyard Haven, MA • Map G5 • 508 693 6071

9 Lenny & Joe's Fish Tale
Famous for clear-broth clam chowder with a touch of milk. ◎ Rte. 1, Westbrook, CT • Map D5 • 860 669 0767

10 Bookstore Restaurant
Oysters don't come fresher. ◎ 50 Kendrick Ave., Wellfleet, MA • Map H4 • 508 349 3154

 Not all seafood restaurants are open year-round. Check before making a special trip.

Left **Antiques shops, Woodbury, CT** Right **Outlet stores, Manchester, VT**

TOP10 **Shopping Destinations**

1 Brimfield, MA
Whether you're seeking Art Deco jewelry or furniture crafted in Salem in the 1790s, Brimfield is the place to look. Antiques hunters from around the world converge on this small town for its three annual antiques shows.
◈ Map D3 • May, Jul, Sep
• www.brimfieldshows.com

2 League of New Hampshire Craftsmen Fair
Established in 1933, the League of New Hampshire Craftsmen Fair is the oldest craft fair in the US. More than 200 juried members of the League offer their work, including jewelry, fine furniture, pottery, and weaving.
◈ Mount Sunapee Resort, Newbury, NH
• Map L5 • Early Aug • Adm
• www.nhcrafts.org

3 Weston, VT
General stores face each other across the main street in this picturesque village. The warren of rooms in the Vermont Country Store contains all kinds of clever gadgets, outdoors apparel, cooking utensils, and a wide selection of New England foods (see p103).

4 Freeport, ME
Outdoors outfitter L. L. Bean set the tone here when it opened in 1911. Freeport has since blossomed as a shopper's paradise;

L. L. Bean, Freeport

more than 170 shops offer the biggest and best name brands in American merchandising – often at substantial discounts. ◈ Map P4 • www.freeportusa.com

Providence Place mega-mall

5 Providence Place, Providence, RI
This mega-mall in downtown Providence has captured most of the retail activity in Rhode Island's retail capital. Stores occupy three levels, with entertainment and a food court above the shops.
◈ One Providence Pl. • Map E4
• www.providenceplace.com

6 Shoppes at Buckland Hills, Manchester, CT
Central Connecticut's largest shopping area, it features virtually every big-box National store, including discount electronics, decor, and home goods dealers like the Christmas Tree Shop. ◈ 194 Buckland Hills Dr. • Map C4 • www. theshoppesatbucklandhills.com

Manchester, VT

Three dozen or so designer outlets with top fashion names like Escada, Tse, and Michael Kors, and home decor ranging from silver tableware to hand-woven Tibetan rugs, make Manchester, Vermont, a Mecca for upscale bargains. ⊗ Map K6
• www.manchesterdesigneroutlets.com

Harvard Square, Cambridge, MA

America's most literary city is home to two comprehensive bookstores, one of which prints out-of-print titles on demand. There are also specialists in used books, poetry, foreign and Marxist literature, and comic books.
⊗ Map F2 • www.harvardsquare.com

Bookshop, Harvard Square

Wellfleet Flea Market & Drive-In, Wellfleet, MA

More than 200 vendors offer a mixture of trash and treasures, including the occasional antique, in the wide-open spaces of a drive-in theater near the end of Cape Cod. ⊗ Rte. 6 • Map H4
• Apr–Oct • Adm • www.wellfleet cinemas.com/flea-market

Woodbury, CT

Dealers in fine US and British antiques set up shop here around half a century ago. They've since been joined by dealers in import porcelain, Oriental rugs, and whatever is giving New York interior decorators shivers this season.
⊗ Map B5 • www.antiqueswoodbury.com

Top 10 Souvenirs

1 Vermont Snow Globe
Capture winter permanently on your knickknack shelf.

2 Tom Brady Bobblehead Doll
The quarterback of the New England Patriots football team is gridiron hero to some, matinee idol to others.

3 Black Dog T-shirt
A black labrador T-shirt says "Martha's Vineyard" to anyone who has ever visited the Black Dog restaurant there.

4 Red Sox Baseball Cap
Show your loyalty in the epic rivalry between the Boston Red Sox and the New York Yankees.

5 Lobster Keychain
The bright crimson of New England's quintessential crustacean makes keys easier to spot.

6 Pine-scented Pillow
Mainers have been selling these fragrant headrests to tourists since steamships started running in the 1830s.

7 "This Car Climbed Mount Washington" Bumper Sticker
People will regard your old clunker with new respect.

8 Nantucket Lightship Basket
True folk art commands high prices for basket-purses with fashion cachet.

9 Woody Jackson "Holy Cow" Calendar
Jackson's art has cornered the market on the iconic black-and-white cows of Vermont.

10 Maine Tourmaline Jewelry
The most famous Western Maine tourmalines are "watermelon" stones with pink centers and green edges.

Left **Patriot's Day** Center **Fourth of July road markings** Right **Thanksgiving Day parade, Plymouth**

🔟 Events

1 WaterFire, Providence, RI
Nothing so epitomizes the renaissance of Providence's waterfront as WaterFire, an award-winning, environmental sculpture by Barnaby Evans. Its 100 floating bonfires, on the city's three downtown rivers, establish a magical setting for a host of summer arts events.
🔍 *Providence, RI • Map E4*
• 401 273 1155 • May–Oct
• Donation • www.waterfire.org

2 Maine Lobster Festival
More than 20,000 lb (9,072 kg) of lobster are steamed every year for this Rockland waterfront festival. Lobstermen race across floating crates, floats parade down the street, and a beauty contest chooses a Sea Goddess to preside over the event.
🔍 *Rockland, ME • Map Q3 • 207 596 0376 • late Jul–early Aug • Adm • www.mainelobsterfestival.com*

Crate race at Maine Lobster Festival

3 Independence Day Celebrations
The red-white-and-blue stripe marks the Fourth of July parade route in Bristol, Rhode Island, site of one of the nation's most fervid small-town parades. Boston's televised Independence Day celebration is famous nationwide for a Boston Pops concert and grand fireworks. 🔍 *Bristol, RI: Map F4; www.july4thbristolri.com • Boston, MA: Map F2; www.july4th.org*

4 Patriot's Day
This reenactment of the opening salvos of the American Revolution starts before dawn in Lexington, Massachusetts, and continues on to nearby Concord.
🔍 *Lexington and Concord, MA • Map F2 • 978 369 6993 • 3rd Mon in Apr • www.nps.gov/mima*

5 Winter Carnival, Stowe, VT
In Stowe, they celebrate falling snow and plummeting temperatures. Snow volleyball, ski-racing, and ice-carving are all part of the fun. 🔍 *Stowe, VT • Map K3 • 802 253 7321 • late Jan • www.stowewintercarnival.com*

6 Jazz and Folk Festivals, Newport, RI
For over 50 years, these festivals have been a focus for fresh talent as well as star performers. Fort Adams State Park is a perfect venue. 🔍 *Newport, RI • Map F5 • Summer • Adm • http://newportjazzfest.net; www.newportfolkfest.net*

Sonny Rollins performing at the 2008 Newport Jazz Festival

Patriot's Day is observed in Massachusetts and Maine (which was once part of Massachusetts).

7 International Festival of Art & Ideas, New Haven, CT

Every June, New Haven bristles with creativity. Hundreds of events, the majority free, include opera on New Haven Green, hip-hop poets, dance, and readings by Nobel Laureate authors. ✆ New Haven, CT • Map C5 • 888 278 4332 • mid-Jun • www.artidea.org

Jack-o'-lanterns, Keene Pumpkin Festival

8 Pumpkin Festival, Keene, NH

Residents and visitors alike bring their pumpkin jack-o'-lanterns to town for the grand display. Each year, more than 20,000 glow against the night sky. ✆ Keene, NH • Map L6 • 603 358 5344 • mid-Oct • www.pumpkinfestival.org

9 Windjammer Days, Boothbay Harbor, ME

Two days of family fun include windjammer cruise schooners and other tall ships in Boothbay Harbor, an antique boat parade, waterfront concerts, a craft fair, and fireworks. ✆ Boothbay Harbor, ME • Map P4 • 207 633 2353 • late Jun • www.boothbayharbor.com

10 Thanksgiving Celebration, Plymouth, MA

Descendents of *Mayflower* pilgrims reenact the Thanksgiving celebration of 1621. A counter ceremony highlights the original Native American culture. ✆ Plymouth, MA • Map G4 • 508 747 7533 • 4th Thu in Nov • www.visit-plymouth.com

Top 10 Agricultural Fairs

1 Eastern States Exposition
New England's largest fair. ✆ 1305 Memorial Ave., W. Springfield, MA • Map C3 • mid-Sep–Oct

2 Fryeburg Fair
This traditional agricultural fair also features woodsmen competitions. ✆ Fryeburg, ME • Map M4 • early Oct

3 Woodstock Fair
Long-established harvest celebration and rural homecoming. ✆ S. Woodstock, CT • Map D4 • late Aug–early Sep

4 Addison County Fair & Field Days
Vermont's largest agricultural fair. ✆ 1790 Field Days Rd., New Haven, VT • Map J4 • early Aug

5 Barnstable County Fair
Demolition derby and bull-riding top the entertainment here. ✆ Rte. 151, E. Falmouth, MA • Map G5 • mid-Jul

6 Washington County Fair
Don't miss the rooster-crowing contest. ✆ Rte. 112, Richmond, RI • Map E5 • mid–late Aug

7 Cheshire Fair
Pony pulls, puppets, pie-eating, and country music. ✆ 247 Monadnock Hwy., Swanzey, NH • Map L6 • late Jul–early Aug

8 Brooklyn Fair
Nashville entertainment, old-fashioned midway rides, and prize poultry. ✆ Rte. 169, Brooklyn, CT • Map D4 • late Aug

9 Champlain Valley Fair
From extreme motorcycle show to sheep and dairy exhibits. ✆ Essex Junction, VT • Map J3 • late Aug–early Sep

10 Topsfield Fair
Farmers have gathered here since 1818. ✆ Topsfield, MA • Map F2 • early Oct

AROUND
NEW
ENGLAND

NEW ENGLAND'S TOP 10

Left **Minute Man National Historic Park, Concord** Right **The cliffs of Aquinnah, Martha's Vineyard**

Massachusetts

Massachusetts is the place where English settlers first imagined remaking their homeland in a wilderness they called New England. For all their English orientation, they called the great bowl of a bay between Cape Cod and the mainland after the coastal "Massachusett" tribe, then took the bay's name for the Massachusetts Bay Colony. The towns of Plymouth, Salem, and Boston – all founded 1620–30 – were the beachhead from which the rest of New England was colonized. As the state with the first college, the first democratic government, the first rebels to defy the king, the first authors to invent an American literature, and the first sailors to open the ports of Asia to the West, Massachusetts can claim that much of what matters about New England happened here first. The state's progressive attitudes and its concentration of colleges and universities keep it on the cutting edge of science and culture to this day.

Faneuil Hall, Boston

Sights

1. Historic Boston
2. Cape Cod
3. Berkshires
4. Salem
5. Lowell
6. New Bedford
7. Concord and Lexington
8. Martha's Vineyard
9. Plymouth
10. Nantucket

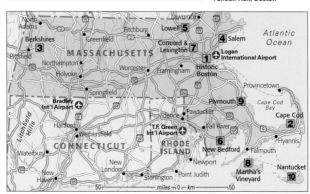

Preceding pages **Old and new buildings juxtaposed in Boston, MA**

Historic Boston

Boston is nicknamed "the Hub," not just because all New England roads do eventually lead here, but because Bostonians think of their home as central to all things historical, intellectual, and cultural in the region. Rightly so; Boston's history is inevitably the lead tale in the anthology of New England's development. As the largest city and the cultural capital, it is the logical place to begin or end a tour of New England *(see pp8–9)*.

Cape Cod

English explorer Bartholomew Gosnold literally put Cape Cod on the map in 1602 when he named the long curl of land for the fish so abundant in its waters. Cape Cod's soils are but 15,000 years old – composed of the sand and gravel that mark the southernmost advance of the last glacier – and it is hardly *terra firma*; every large storm subtly reshapes the shoreline, making peninsulas into islands and vice versa. Yet the very transience of Cape Cod is part of its allure *(see pp12–13)*.

The boardwalk at Sandwich, Cape Cod

Berkshires

Almost equidistant from Boston to the east and New York City to the south, the Berkshire Hills of western Massachusetts pledge a wavering allegiance to both. But the Berkshires is a valley kingdom unto itself. Its busy summer social schedule revolves around the performing arts, but the concentration of resident artists and performers guarantees a rich off-season as well *(see pp26–7)*.

Salem Witch Museum

Salem

In the popular imagination, Salem is the city that tried and executed witches. But the 1692 trials are best regarded as an aberration in the history of this vibrant, entrepreneurial city blessed with the magnificent art of the Peabody Essex Museum *(see p45)* and a rich maritime history recounted at the Salem Maritime National Historic Site *(see p35)*. In the early days of the country, Salem's merchant princes were richer than the national treasury. Their magnificent houses still attest to their power and glory. ✪ *Map F2*

Lowell

Lowell was the first purpose-built city in the US, constructed in the 1820s as a large-scale factory town to manufacture textiles with equipment designs adapted from British mills. The textile industry is gone, but the canal network and looming mills remain as testament to America's first engagement with the Industrial Revolution *(see p32)*. After you've soaked up the mill history, visit Jack Kerouac Park (part of Lowell National Historical Park) to pay your respects to the Beat author who was a native son. ✪ *Map E2*

Witch Trials

Salem exhibits mixed feelings about its witch history. On the 300th anniversary of the 1692 hysteria that led to the hanging of 19 "witches" and crushing of another, the city erected a solemn memorial to the victims. But come Halloween, Salem is "witch city," capitalizing on its sensational past to draw curious visitors.

New Bedford

6 Settled in 1640, this deepwater port at the mouth of Buzzards Bay has always wrested its living from the sea. In the 1840s, pine-masted whaling barks would tie up at the wharves to offload precious whale oil from a three-year journey *(see p34)*. Today that harbor creaks with great iron fishing boats that dredge the bay for scallops, haul flounder from Nantucket Shoals, or venture far offshore for cod and haddock. Somehow the sea air tastes saltiest here. ◈ *Map F4*

Replica of the original *Mayflower*, Plymouth

voices in Ralph Waldo Emerson (1803–82) and Henry David Thoreau (1817–62). Other writers and thinkers who called Concord home include novelists Nathaniel Hawthorne (1804–64) and Louisa May Alcott (1832–88), who grew up in Orchard House *(see p52)*. All of the above are buried at Concord's Sleepy Hollow Cemetery. ◈ *Map F2 • Ralph Waldo Emerson House: 28 Cambridge Tpk., Concord; 978 369 2236; Open mid-Apr– Oct: 10am–4:30pm Thu–Sat, 1–4:30pm Sun; adm*

Fishing boats, New Bedford

Concord and Lexington

7 The opening skirmishes of the American Revolution, in what is now Minute Man National Historical Park *(see p33)*, forever link these neighboring towns. More than words of war, Concord also gave the US its first literary

Martha's Vineyard

8 Covering 100 sq miles (259 sq km) yet only 7 miles (11 km) off the mainland, the flounder-shaped island of Martha's Vineyard is big enough that you'll want a car to explore its very different communities. Up Island – the rustic western end – is a serene natural world that includes the sacred striped clay banks of Aquinnah. Down Island – the bustling eastern end – has the town of Vineyard Haven, the old whaling port of Edgartown, and the camp-meeting resort of Oak Bluffs. ◈ *Map G5*

For more on New England's maritime history **See pp34–5**

Plymouth

Plymouth calls itself "America's home town," as it was the first English settlement in New England and home of the Separatists, who became known as Pilgrims. The living history museum of Plimoth Plantation *(see p32)* depicts the settlement circa 1627, and also has exhibits devoted to Wampanoag life in the same era. History is marked with a statue or plaque on almost every corner of pleasant modern Plymouth. Pilgrim Hall Museum displays artifacts of the original Pilgrims, and addresses some distortions of their story.

Map G5 • Pilgrim Hall Museum: 75 Court St., Plymouth; 508 746 1620; Open Feb–Dec: 9:30am–4:30pm daily; adm; www.pilgrimhall.org

Nantucket

In contrast with Martha's Vineyard, only residents bother to bring a car to tiny Nantucket, as the island lies 30 miles (48 km) offshore and transport is expensive. Even residents tend to bicycle everywhere (tourists on scooters are scorned). Explore venerable gray-shingled Nantucket town on foot, stopping first at the whaling museum *(see p34)*. Then bike out to Wauwinet to hike the dunes at Great Point, to 'Sconset to see rose-covered cottages, or Surfside to swim or fly kites on the beach. Map G5

Nantucket Whaling Museum

A Day Pedaling from Cambridge to Concord

Morning

Start your 13-mile (21-km) jaunt through American history by taking your bike with you on the T to the Alewife terminus of the Red Line. Follow well-marked signs to the **Minuteman Bikeway**, a flat, paved path. Pedal through Arlington, then watch for egrets, herons, and bobolinks along the edges of **Great Meadows** nature area. The bikeway soon passes the Lexington visitor center of **Minute Man National Historical Park**, perfect for a rest stop. Pick up the park map and brochures, taking note of historic **Lexington Green**, your next stop. Make a silent salute to the iconic Minute Man statue on the green, then pedal a few blocks up Bedford Street to enjoy big deli sandwiches at **Neillio's Gourmet Kitchen**.

Afternoon

Just west of Lexington Green you switch from the Minuteman Bikeway to **Battle Road Trail**, an unpaved road for walkers and cyclists that parallels the route of the running battle as British forces retreated in 1775; historical signposts explain the significance of sights along the way. **North Bridge**, near another visitor center in the park, is especially evocative. At the end of the trail, follow signs to **The Wayside** and **Orchard House** *(see p52)* to learn about Concord's 19th-century literary history. Lexington Rd. takes you into Concord Center, where you and your bike can return to Boston on the commuter rail.

Lexington Green is where the American Revolution began. British soldiers and American militia met here on April 19, 1775.

Left **Mohawk Trail** Center **Historic houses, Old Deerfield** Right **Furniture, Worcester Art Museum**

TOP 10 Best of the Rest

1 Gloucester
Sticking 30 miles (42 km) out to sea on Cape Ann, Gloucester's busy harbor is a legendary fishing port and home to Rocky Neck Art Colony (see p76). ◎ Map G2

2 Rockport
Iconic Motif #1, a red fishing shed in the harbor, is among the most-painted subjects in this lovely village filled with art galleries and boutiques. ◎ Map G2

3 Deerfield and the Connecticut Valley
Settlers braved frequent Indian raids for the rich soil of the Connecticut Valley. Historic Deerfield preserves 60 buildings from the 17th and 18th centuries. ◎ Map C2 • Historic Deerfield: The Street, Old Deerfield; 413 774 5581; open mid-Apr–Nov: 9:30am–4:30pm daily; Dec–mid-Apr: call for hours; adm; www.historic-deerfield.org

4 Springfield
Once your kids have climbed on the Dr Seuss statues at the Quadrangle off State St., take them to visit the nearby history, art, and natural science museums. ◎ Map C3 • 800 625 7738 • www.springfieldmuseums.org

5 Northampton and Amherst
The vibrant cultural life of Pioneer Valley revolves around four colleges, including Smith, with its major art museum (see p48). Literary history abounds, as the Emily Dickinson Homestead (see p52) attests. ◎ Map C3

6 Mohawk Trail
Drive Route 2 west from Greenfield over the Berkshire Mountains to North Adams to be wowed by some of New England's best fall foliage. Turnoffs lead to orchards and sugar houses. ◎ Map C2 • www.mohawktrail.com

7 Ipswich and Essex
The long sands of Crane Beach (see p42) in Ipswich and the winding tidal river at Essex (see p76) make these North Shore communities tops for nature lovers. Both are renowned for local shellfish. ◎ Map F2, G2

8 Newburyport
Its fantastic concentration of grand Federal-style homes makes Newburyport an essential stop for history buffs and preservationists. Birders flock to Plum Island at harbor mouth for some of New England's best birding. ◎ Map F1

9 Worcester
Worcester has a first-rate art museum (see p44) and a unique museum of arms and armor, the Higgins Armory. ◎ Map E3 • Higgins Armory: 100 Barber Av., Worcester; 508 853 6015; 10am–4pm Tue–Sat, noon–4pm Sun; adm; www.higgins.org

10 Brimfield and Sturbridge
New England's rural heart bustles three times a year with Brimfield antiques shows (see p62). Old Sturbridge Village (see p32) re-creates rural New England of 150 years ago. ◎ Map D3

Visit Virgilio's at 29 Main St., Gloucester, to taste the St Joseph roll sandwich invented for local fishermen.

Left **Boston Symphony Orchestra, Tanglewood** Right **Panic at the Disco, Bank of America Pavilion**

🔟 Summer Performing Arts

1 Tanglewood
Supreme musicianship and elaborate picnics are equally characteristic of the Boston Symphony's summer home. *297 West St., Lenox • Map B3 • 413 637 1600 • late Jun–early Sep • Adm • www.bso.org*

2 Jacob's Pillow Dance Festival
Enjoy performances by leading US and international dance companies in a magical setting. *358 George Carter Rd., Becket • Map B3 • 413 243 9919 • mid-Jun–late Aug • Adm • www.jacobspillow.org*

3 Shakespeare & Company
Famed for their Shakespeare performances, this company also develops and produces new plays of social and political significance. *70 Kemble St., Lenox • Map B3 • 413 637 1199 • late May–mid Sep • Adm • www.shakespeare.org*

4 Barrington Stage Company
A wellspring of new plays and musicals, Barrington Stage incubates electrifying theater that often winds up on Broadway. *30 Union St., Pittsfield • Map B2 • 413 236 8888 • mid-Jun–Oct • Adm • www.barringtonstageco.org*

5 Gloucester Stage Company
Home is a former fish-packing plant adjacent to Rocky Neck Art Colony. Award-winning playwright Israel Horowitz is a company co-founder. *267 E. Main St., Gloucester • Map G2 • 978 281 4433 • Jun–Aug • Adm • www.gloucesterstage.org*

6 Wellfleet Harbor Actors Theater
Humor, passion, a sense of the absurd, and a sharp political edge are hallmarks of this small troupe. *Rte. 6, Wellfleet • Map H4 • 508 349 9428 • May–Oct • Adm • www.what.org*

7 Cape Playhouse
The country's oldest professional summer theater entertains with a mix of classics, comedies, mysteries, and musicals. *820 Rte. 6A, Dennis • Map H4 • 508 385 3911 • mid-Jun–Oct, 2nd half Dec • Adm • www.capeplayhouse.com*

8 Berkshire Theatre Festival
The 1888 Stockbridge Casino by noted architect Stanford White makes a grand setting for new, classic, and contemporary theater. *Main St., Stockbridge • Map B3 • 413 298 5576 • mid-Jun–mid-Sep • Adm • www.berkshiretheatre.org*

9 Williamstown Theatre Festival
Film and TV directors and actors come here to hone their stagecraft; celebrity-spotting is summer sport in town. *1000 Main St., Williamstown • Map B2 • 413 597 3400 • Jun–Aug • Adm • www.wtfestival.org*

10 Bank of America Pavilion
This harborside pavilion is a dynamic venue for a wide range of performers. *290 Northern Ave., Boston • Map F3 • 617 728 1600 • Jun–early Sep • Adm • www.livenation.com/bank-of-america-pavilion-tickets-boston/venue/8310*

See the Sunday edition of the Boston Globe *for detailed arts listings.*

Left **Regattabar** Right **Middle East**

🔟 Bars and Nightlife in Boston

1 Via Matta
Arrive early if you want to see the sleek northern-Italian styling of the Via Matta bar. At night it's packed with beautiful people sipping cocktails and munching bruschetta. ✆ *79 Park Plaza • Map V4*

2 Dante
Ever wonder where high-tech geniuses unwind? Every day from 4–6pm the bar at this posh Cambridge restaurant offers cocktail specials and $1 oysters on the half-shell. ✆ *Sonesta Hotel, 40 Edwin Land Blvd., Cambridge • Map U2*

3 Regattabar
This intimate room with fine acoustics is widely acclaimed for presenting some of the best jazz in the US. ✆ *Charles Hotel, 1 Bennett St., Cambridge • Map F2*

4 Beehive
This Bohemian bar-café programs live jazz by local artists. The imaginative bistro menu is complemented by exotic champagne cocktails. ✆ *541 Tremont St. • Map V5*

5 Nick's Comedy Stop
Nationally-known comics from HBO, Showtime, Comedy Central, MTV, and the like headline at Boston's longest-running comedy club. ✆ *100 Warrenton St. • Map V4*

6 Kinsale Irish Pub & Restaurant
Built in Ireland, then shipped to Boston and re-assembled, the Kinsale is an authentic piece of the old sod. There's live music on Tuesday and Saturday. ✆ *2 Center Plaza, Cambridge St. • Map W3*

7 Middle East
If you follow underground music, you are probably already aware of this legendary venue for new bands looking to break through. ✆ *472–480 Massachusetts Ave., Cambridge • Map S3*

8 Drink
Fresh herbs, hand-chipped ice, and specialty liqueurs place this utterly hip bar in the vanguard of the cocktail world. Bartenders ask your mood then improvise a drink. ✆ *348 Congress St. • Map X4*

9 Game On
Sports-crazy Boston's top bar is built into the walls of Fenway Park. With an entire wall covered with flat-screen TVs, there's always, well, a game on. ✆ *82 Lansdowne St. • Map S5*

10 House of Blues®
The famed performance chain sticks to its Boston roots with this cavernous venue. ✆ *15 Lansdowne St. • Map S5*

Last call at Boston bars is usually half an hour before closing time.

Price Categories

For a three course meal for one with half a bottle of wine (or equivalent meal), taxes and extra charges.

$	under $25
$$	$25–$40
$$$	$40–$50
$$$$	$50–$65
$$$$$	over $65

Left **Locke-Ober** Right **B+G Oysters**

🔟 Restaurants in Boston

Clio
If cuisine is art, chef-owner Ken Orringer is its Picasso. Plan on a long, sumptuous evening. ◎ 370-A Commonwealth Ave., Boston, MA • Map T5 • 617 536 7200 • Closed L, Sun • $$$$$

Petit Robert Bistro
Whether you crave a hotdog with cheese, a bowl of onion soup, or coq au vin with buttered noodles, great Parisian comfort food awaits. ◎ 468 Commonwealth Ave. • Map S5 • 617 375 0699 • $$

B+G Oysters
At least a dozen varieties of oyster are available here, with sparkling and mineral-rich white wines to match. ◎ 550 Tremont St. • Map V5 • 617 423 0550 • $$$$

Hamersley's Bistro
French country cooking with contemporary panache uses local meat, produce, and seafood. ◎ 553 Tremont St. • Map V5 • 617 423 2700 • Closed L, open Sun brunch • $$$$$

Locke-Ober
A gourmet stalwart since the 1890s, Locke-Ober serves modern interpretations of Escoffier's culinary canon. ◎ 3 Winter Place • Map W4 • 617 543 1340 • Closed Sun • $$$$$

L'Espalier
Come here for impeccable prix-fixe French *haute cuisine* with a New England twist. ◎ 774 Boylston St. • Map U5 • 617 351 2037 • $$$$$

East Coast Grill
Hit dishes at this colorful joint include grilled fish with fiery salsas, BBQ-pulled pork, and ice-cold oysters washed down with margaritas. ◎ 1271 Cambridge St., Cambridge • Map S1 • 617 491 6568 • Closed L, open Sun brunch • $$$

Rialto
The chef-owner of this sophisticated dining room in Harvard Square makes field trips delving into regional cuisines of Italy then magically recreates them with local ingredients. ◎ 1 Bennett St., Cambridge • Map F2 • 617 661 5050 • Closed L • $$$$$

Mare
A fish-lover's dream, Mare specializes in Italian coastal cuisines with an eco emphasis. ◎ 135 Richmond St. • Map X3 • 617 723 6273 • Closed L • $$$$

Tremont 647
This small, rocking restaurant offers a lively bar scene and adventurous food. Neighborhood foodies adore the weekend pajama brunches. ◎ 647 Tremont St. • Map U6 • 617 226 4600 • Closed L Mon–Fri • $$$

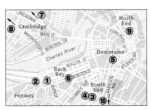

Left **Faneuil Hall Marketplace** Right **Yankee Candle Village**

Places to Shop in Massachusetts

1 Faneuil Hall Marketplace
Dozens of boutiques and specialty shops dot North and South Markets. Quincy Market has the city's best food court, as well as more than 40 pushcart vendors selling largely local wares. ⊗ *Boston • Map X3*

2 Fuller Craft Museum
This premier museum of fine art in craft media carries an extensive selection of artists' jewelry, as well as work in glass, ceramic, fiber, and wood. ⊗ *455 Oak St., Brockton • Map F3*

3 The Store @ DeCordova
Contemporary art, mostly by New England artists, is the focus of DeCordova Museum & Sculpture Park. The museum store matches that spirit with art supplies, jewelry, wearable art, and inventive educational toys. ⊗ *51 Sandy Pond Rd., Lincoln • Map F2*

4 Wrentham Village Premium Outlets
Bargain hunters from all over New England converge on this mall just off I-495 for 170 stores dedicated to designer apparel and upscale housewares. ⊗ *1 Premium Outlets Blvd., Wrentham • Map F3*

5 Rocky Neck Art Colony
It's easy to see why this rocky peninsula is such an inspiration to artists. You can walk from cottage to cottage to see (and buy) paintings by resident painters. ⊗ *Map G2*

6 Yankee Candle Village
The leading US producer of scented candles offers the world's largest candle selection, home furnishings, food, entertainment, all-year Christmas shopping, and a candle-making museum. ⊗ *Rtes. 5 & 10, South Deerfield • Map C2*

7 Sandwich Glass Museum
The museum shop carries faithful reproductions of historic pressed glass from Sandwich, an extensive line of American art glass, and blown glass from the museum's own glass studio. ⊗ *129 Main St., Sandwich • Map G4*

8 Essex
More than 30 antiques shops do business in this historic North Shore community. Look sharply to find nautical artifacts, Chinese export porcelain, 18th- and 19th-century furniture, and excellent oil paintings. ⊗ *Map G2*

9 Provincetown
In summer, Friday is "gallery night" in Provincetown. Galleries along Commercial Street set out wine and cheese to lure prospective buyers. ⊗ *Map H3*

10 Paradise City Arts Festivals
Two of New England's largest gatherings of crafts artists and designers take place over Memorial Day (late May) and Columbus Day (mid-Oct) weekends at Northampton's Tri-County Fairgrounds. ⊗ *Rte. 9 and Old Ferry Rd., Northampton • Map C3*

Massachusetts sales tax does not apply to most items of clothing.

Price Categories

For a three course meal for one with half a bottle of wine (or equivalent meal), taxes and extra charges.

$	under $25
$$	$25–$40
$$$	$40–$50
$$$$	$50–$65
$$$$$	over $65

Wheatleigh Hotel, Lenox

Restaurants in Massachusetts

Chillingsworth
Fine French *haute cuisine* has made this Cape Cod restaurant a legend. ✆ 2449 Main St., Brewster, MA • Map H4 • 508 896 3640 • Closed Mon, Fri–Sun L, Dec–Apr • $$$$$

Wheatleigh Hotel
Elegant country dining fit for an English baron with French taste. ✆ 11 Hawthorne Rd., Lenox, MA • Map B3 • 413 637 0610 • Closed L, Wed • $$$$$

Left Bank, Stonehedge Inn
Enjoy lively seasonal cuisine, sourced locally, and the best wine cellar in New England. Bargain monthly wine dinners pair courses with wines from a single producer. ✆ 160 Pawtucket Blvd., Tyngsboro • Map E2 • 978 649 4400 • Open for B, L, D daily, brunch Sun • $$$$$

Back Eddy
Cutting-edge casual cuisine with a raw bar of Westport shellfish and succulent wood-grilled local meats and fish. The outdoor bar is the most convivial summer social scene on Massachusetts' south coast. ✆ 1 Bridge Rd., Westport • Map F4 • 508 636 6500 • Closed Mon–Fri L, Jan–Mar • $$$$

Topper's
In an idyllic waterfront setting, dine on Beef Wellington, skillet-roasted halibut, or buttered lobster with tortellini in a truffle emulsion. ✆ 120 Wauwinet Rd., Nantucket • Map H5 • 508 228 0145 • Closed late Oct–Apr • $$$$$

Sweet Life Café
The contemporary French menu of seafood and vegetables and the Bordeaux-dominated wine list betray the owner's Gallic origins. ✆ 63 Circuit Ave., Oak Bluffs, Martha's Vineyard • Map G5 • 508 696 0200 • Closed L, Mon–Wed May & Sep–Oct, Nov–Apr • $$$$$

Duckworth's Bistrot
The French-trained chef-owner offers sumptuous bistro fare – grilled strip steak, duck breast with apples, and seafood stew. ✆ 197 E. Main St., Gloucester • Map G2 • 978 282 4426 • Closed L, Mon, Sun Sep–May, Jan • $$$$

Il Capriccio
The elegant Northern Italian menu changes frequently, depending on the New England harvest and the fishermen's catch. There's an extensive wine list. ✆ 888 Main St., Waltham • Map F2 • 781 894 2234 • Closed L, Sun • $$$$

Castle Street Cafe
Really taste the Berkshires at this local favorite where the chef offers a superb bar menu of classic bistro dishes. ✆ 10 Castle St., Great Barrington • Map B3 • 413 528 5244 • Closed L, Sun (Nov–Jan) • $$$

Blue Ginger
Food Network superstar Ming Tsai's home kitchen blends Asian and Western influences in light, spicy, innovative dishes. ✆ 585 Washington St., Wellesley • Map F3 • 781 283 5790 • Closed Sun L • $$$$$

All restaurants open for lunch and dinner daily unless indicated. Reservations are usually essential for all of the above.

Left **Rhode Island State House, Providence** Right **Wetland wildlife refuge, Charlestown**

Rhode Island

Rhode Island is not an island at all, but it claims more than its share of dramatic rocky cliffs, sandy beaches, and languid riverbanks. The state was founded by religious dissenters from Massachusetts who chafed at the orthodoxies of Boston and Salem Puritans. The smallest US state, Rhode Island is divided by the very large, fan-shaped Narragansett Bay. At the head of the bay, the capital city of Providence revels in both its Colonial history and its futuristic outlook – the latter courtesy of its colleges and universities. The South County coastline west of the bay features idyllic barrier beaches with long, golden strands and fertile marshes trapped behind high dunes. The mouth of the bay is crossed by stepping-stone islands (and some magnificent bridges) that lead to the first home of the US Navy, now the yachting capital of Newport.

Newport harbor and the Claiborne Pell Bridge

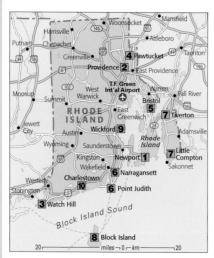

Preceding pages **The pier, Old Orchard Beach, Maine**

1 Newport
Nineteenth-century mansions and a snug harbor dotted with speedboats and racing yachts make Newport one of the great summer destinations. The downtown area is a history buff's delight *(see pp14–15)*.

2 Providence
Rhode Island School of Design (RISD) *(see pp48, 87)*, a premier US art school, provides zing to downtown Providence, a city also known as a major dining destination. Benefit Street's "Mile of History" captures in its museums and historic houses two-and-a-half centuries of New England life. Savor a cannoli and visit the galleries of Federal Hill on the West Side, a traditionally Italian district now developing a major art scene. ◎ *Map E4*

3 Watch Hill
The glorious beaches of South County, the Rhode Island shore west of Point Judith, reach their apogee at Watch Hill, an old-fashioned seaside community of the town of Westerly. The village also boasts the charming Flying Horse Carousel *(see p51)*. ◎ *Map E5*

4 Pawtucket
So close to Providence that it can be hard to distinguish the two cities, Pawtucket flourished because it sits at the mouth of the Blackstone River, the storied

Slater Mill, Pawtucket

stream of 19th-century industry that drains central New England. It was here that in 1793, Samuel Slater opened the country's first successful cotton mill *(see p33)*, jump-starting the American Industrial Revolution. Today it is best known for the minor-league Pawtucket Red Sox *(see p84)*, and its Dragon Boat Race in September. ◎ *Map E4*

Independence Day celebrations, Bristol

5 Bristol
Renowned for exuberant Independence Day celebrations that date from 1785 *(see p64)*, Bristol is a charming deep-water seaport on the east side of Narragansett Bay. The village is home to the Herreshoff yacht-building firm, whose museum also traces the history of the America's Cup, the most prestigious prize in yacht-racing. Visit the house and gardens of the Blithewold estate, where Rhode Island brides flock to wed with spectacular vistas of Narragansett Bay as a backdrop. ◎ *Map F4*
• *Herreshoff Marine Museum: 1 Burnside St.; 401 253 5000; open Apr–mid-Dec: 10am–5pm daily; adm; www.herreshoff. org* • *Blithewold Mansion & Gardens: 101 Ferry Rd.; 401 253 2707; open mid-Apr–mid-Oct: 10am–4pm Wed–Sat (to 3pm Sun); adm; www.blithewold.org*

Most of the houses on Benefit Street, Providence, display plaques identifying who built them and when.

What a span!

Constructed 1966–9, Newport's Claiborne Pell Bridge is not only the longest bridge in Rhode Island, it's also the largest suspension bridge in New England. With a main span of 1,601 ft (488 m) and an overall length of 11,247 ft (3,428 m), the bridge arcs over Narragansett Bay to connect Jamestown and Newport.

Narragansett/Point Judith

In 1900, a fire destroyed the fancy hotels and casino that made Narragansett Beach a high-society resort. Today, families and sunbathers rule the beach while surfers ride the waves. The peninsula leading south ends at Point Judith, which shelters the busy fishing port of Galilee. Whale-watch and deep-sea-fishing cruise vessels share berths with the fishing boats. Don't miss fish dinner at George's of Galilee *(see p61)*. ◈ *Map E5*

Tiverton/Little Compton

Occupying their own little peninsula between Narragansett Bay and the Massachusetts border, Tiverton *(see p38)* and Little Compton are insulated from

Sakonnet Vineyards, Little Compton

the modern world by woods and rolling farmland. Watch for roadside stands selling seasonal strawberries and sweet corn. Wine grapes also flourish. Visit Sakonnet Vineyards for tours and tastings. One of New England's largest wineries, Sakonnet has switched from French-American hybrid grapes to European varietals. Its *gewürztraminer* is a standout. ◈ *Map F4, F5 • Sakonnet Vineyards: 162 W Main Rd., Little Compton; 800 919 4637; open late May–mid-Oct: 10am–6pm daily; mid-Oct–late May: 11am–5pm; www.sakonnetwine.com*

Mohegan Bluffs, Block Island

Block Island

Just 13 miles (21 km) off the coast, Block Island has long been a summer vacation haven for New Englanders. A quarter of its land is protected against development (zoning prohibits modern structures), and 30 miles (48 km) of nature trails crisscross the pear-shaped island. Crescent Beach, just north of the Victorian resort village of Old Harbor, has fabulous swimming and – when the wind is right – good surfing. Deep-sea-fishing excursions are popular day-trips from Old Harbor. ◈ *Map E6 • Block Island Ferry: Pt. Judith; 401 783 7996; www.blockislandferry.com*

Wickford Harbor

Wickford

Artists and craftspeople have flocked to this salty village of the town of North Kingstown, and their galleries and shops (along with the picturesque, deeply historic village itself) are big lures for daytrippers from Providence and the Connecticut coast. What few visitors realize is that Wickford's location on the west side of Narragansett Bay makes it the ideal launching point for exploring the bay by sea kayak. Inquire about expert guided paddles at the Kayak Centre of Rhode Island. ◈ *Map E5*
• *Kayak Centre of Rhode Island: 9 Phillips St., 401 295 4400; daily year-round; adm; www.kayakcentre.com*

Charlestown

It can be hard to tell whether Charlestown is land or water, as the 4-mile (6.4-km) coastline encompasses the largest saltwater marshes in the state. You'll find some of New England's best birding for wading birds and waterfowl in this watery ecosystem between land and sea. Sprawling Ninigret Park has tracks for cyclists and bladers as well as a swimming pool and tennis courts. Every clear Friday night, join the astronomy buffs at Frosty Drew Observatory to scan the skies. ◈ *Map E5* • *Frosty Drew Observatory: 61 Park Ln., Ninigret Park; 401 364 9508; open clear Fri nights, year-round; www. frostydrew.org*

A Stroll Through Providence History

Morning

In 1994, Providence re-claimed the once-industrial banks of its river with the linear park called the **River Walk**. Start your stroll at **Waterplace Park,** a broad pool and amphitheater between Francis and Exchange streets. Cross the **Steeple Street Bridge**, noting the soaring Ionic columns of the **First Baptist Church in America** on the left. To tide you over until a late lunch, pop into **Cafe Choklad** (2 Thomas St.) for hot chocolate and brioche before climbing the hill to **Benefit Street**. Make your first stop on the hill at the fabulous **RISD Museum**. On Benefit Street you'll pass the Greek Revival **Providence Athenaeum**, where macabre master storyteller Edgar Allan Poe courted Sarah Whitman.

Afternoon

When you reach the corner of Power Street (no.52), you'll finally get to go inside one of the manses – now the **John Brown House Museum**, built in Georgian style in 1786, and the most lavish Providence home of its day. The impeccable restoration shows Brown's luxurious furnishings as well as the cozier, less ostentatious tastes of succeeding generations. The family founded **Brown University**, where you can shake out the cobwebs of the past on Thayer Street, a short walk northeast. You've earned that late lunch, so join the youthful masses for pasta, pizza, or a burger at **Cafe Paragon** (234 Thayer St.) before you hit the shops.

Around New England – Rhode Island

The First Baptist Church in America was built in 1774–5, but the congregation was founded in 1638, by theologian Roger Williams.

83

Left **Green Animals Topiary Garden** Center **Museum of Work and Culture** Right **Pawtucket Red Sox**

TOP 10 Best of the Rest

1 Audubon Society of Rhode Island Environmental Education Center

Explore marine life at this family-friendly wildlife refuge. ◈ *1401 Hope St., Rte. 114, Bristol • Map F4 • 401 245 7500 • Open daily • Adm • www.asri.org*

2 Beavertail Lighthouse Museum

There's been a lighthouse here since 1749. The keeper's house is now a museum. ◈ *Beavertail State Park, Jamestown • Map E5 • 401 423 3270 • Open Jun–early Sep daily; Oct Sat & Sun • Adm • www.beavertaillight.org*

3 Casey Farm

This 18th-century farmhouse offers a glimpse into Rhode Island's agricultural past. Produce grown here is sold on Saturdays. ◈ *2325 Boston Neck Rd., Saunderstown (North Kingstown) • Map E5 • 401 295 1030 • Open Jun–mid-Oct Tue, Thu & Sat • Adm*

4 Green Animals Topiary Garden

A Rhode Island Red rooster is one of the 80 topiaries at the US's oldest topiary garden. ◈ *380 Cory's Lane, off Rte. 114, Portsmouth • Map F5 • 401 847 1000 • Open late May–early Oct daily • Adm • www.newportmansions.org*

5 City Center Ice Rink

Skate in the shadow of Rhode Island's tallest skyscraper – the 428-ft (130-m) Art Deco "Superman Building." ◈ *2 Kennedy Plaza, Providence • Map E4 • 401 331 5544 • Open late Nov–early Mar daily • Adm • www. kennedyplaza.org/skating-information*

6 Pawtuxet Village

A mid-June parade marks the 1772 burning of a British ship by local patriots. Dozens of Colonial buildings feature in the historic district. ◈ *Warwick • Map E4*

7 Museum of Work and Culture

This museum in a former textile mill details the lives of those who worked here and in other local factories. ◈ *42 S. Main St., Woonsocket • Map E3 • 401 769 9675 • Closed Mon • Adm • www.rihs.org*

8 Gilbert Stuart Birthplace and Museum

Artist Gilbert Stuart (1755–1828) painted the celebrities of his day. A tour here uncovers his modest beginnings. ◈ *815 Gilbert Stuart Rd., Saunderstown • Map E5 • 401 294 3001 • Open May–mid-Oct Thu–Mon • Adm • www.gilbertstuartmuseum.org*

9 East Bay Bike Path

Zip down the bayside path between East Providence and Bristol for views of Narragansett Bay on one side, herons and egrets on the other. ◈ *Map F4*

10 Pawtucket Red Sox Baseball, McCoy Stadium

Many top baseball players perfected their game with this Boston Triple-A team. Grab a seat in McCoy Stadium and you might spot the next rising star. ◈ *1 Columbus Ave., Pawtucket • Map E4 • 401 724 7300 • Open Apr–Sep • Adm • www.pawsox.com*

Price Categories

For a three course meal for one with half a bottle of wine (or equivalent meal), taxes and extra charges.

$	under $25
$$	$25–$40
$$$	$40–$50
$$$$	$50–$65
$$$$$	over $65

Left **Le Central** Right **New Rivers**

🔟 Restaurants

White Horse Tavern
America's oldest tavern (since 1673) offers classic American cuisine in a setting of beamed ceilings, log fires, and candlelit tables. ◈ *26 Marlborough St., Newport • Map F5 • 401 849 3600 • Closed Sun L; open Sun brunch • $$$$$*

Le Central
East Bay (as in Narragansett) meets Left Bank (as in Paris) at this French bistro with a short menu of excellent comfort food (such as cassoulet with duck confit) and spectacular local fish. ◈ *483 Hope St., Bristol • Map F4 • 401 396 9965 • Closed Sun–Mon • $$$*

Trio
Trio serves chops, pasta, and seafood at bargain prices. Dig into a juicy rib-eye steak, basil rigatoni, or pan-seared scallops. ◈ *15 Kingstown Rd., Narragansett • Map E5 • 401 792 4333 • $$$*

Al Forno
Baked pastas and meats roasted in a wood-fired oven have brought Al Forno fame as one of the best casual restaurants in the US. ◈ *577 S. Main St., Providence • Map E4 • 401 273 9760 • Closed Sun, Mon, Tue–Sat L • $$$$*

Wright's Farm Restaurant
This 1,000-seater is the best of the Rhode Island "all-you-can-eat chicken dinner" restaurants. ◈ *84 Inman Rd., Harrisville • Map E4 • 401 769 2856 • Closed Mon–Fri L, Mon–Wed D • $*

New Rivers
Spicy contemporary cooking at its best pairs with an intimate dining space for a truly romantic experience. ◈ *7 Steeple St., Providence • Map E4 • 401 751 0350 • Closed L, Sun D • $$$$*

Chez Pascal
The chef-owner of this unabashedly Burgundian bistro makes his own pâtés, sausages, and confits. Share a charcuterie appetizer followed by the pork of the day. ◈ *960 Hope St., Providence • Map E4 • 401 421 4422 • Closed L, Sun • $$$$*

Castle Hill Inn
Enjoy fine local seafood and sweeping views of Narragansett Bay at this high-class Newport dining room. ◈ *590 Ocean Dr., Newport • Map F5 • 401 849 3800 • Closed Sun L; open Sun brunch • $$$$$*

Atlantic Inn
The four-course, fixed-price dinners are the star attraction here. Prized verandah tables have spectacular sunset views. ◈ *High St., Block Island • Map E6 • 401 466 5883 • Closed late Apr–late May & Sep–late Oct Mon–Wed D; L all year • $$$$*

Bridge
Take a detour to this top downtown destination for creative US cuisine. The focus is on local food, and in particular fresh, native seafood. ◈ *37 Main St., Westerly • Map E5 • 401 348 9700 • $$$*

Most of these restaurants serve scallops and line-caught fish landed at Galilee. All open for lunch and dinner daily unless indicated.

Left **Perks & Corks** Right **Trinity Brewhouse**

TOP 10 Cafés and Bars

Perks & Corks
1 By day, Perks & Corks is a slacker's dream of a coffee bar, with smooth lattes, free Wi-Fi, and enveloping sofas. After dark it morphs into a bar with wines by the glass and killer cocktails.
⬡ *48 High St., Westerly • Map E5*

Chan's Fine Oriental Dining
2 Known for its "eggroll jazz," Chan's hops on the weekends when blues bands and small jazz combos set the diners' fingers snapping. The Chinese fare draws on several regional cuisines.
⬡ *267 Main St., Woonsocket • Map E3*

Fluke Wine, Bar & Kitchen
3 Catch the sunset from this atmospheric bar on Newport Harbor, while enjoying a glass of chardonnay with a bowl of steamed clams. ⬡ *41 Bowen's Wharf, Newport • Map F5*

Costantino's Venda Ravioli
4 This Italian gourmet shop, with a huge selection of pastas, cheeses, and sausages, also serves coffee and food at tables in the back. ⬡ *265 Atwells Ave., Providence • Map E4*

Trinity Brewhouse
5 Trinity is a "United Nations" of beer; its ales, lagers, and stout made on the premises recall English, German, and Irish styles. It's a popular after-show venue with playgoers at Trinity Repertory Theatre. ⬡ *186 Fountain St., Providence • Map E4*

Olympia Tea Room
6 Score one of the outdoor tables at this delightful spot near the Flying Horses Carousel, and you can watch the action while you sip white wine and lunch on roasted clams with linguine.
⬡ *74 Bay St., Watch Hill • Map E5*

Scales & Shells
7 After the dinner rush, this all-fish restaurant turns into a convivial bar, where patrons can enjoy local shellfish from the raw bar with their wine and beer.
⬡ *527 Thames St., Newport • Map F5*

George's of Galilee
8 Stop off here to savor the pick of the catch from the Galilee fishermen; many spend their evenings at the bar. ⬡ *250 Sand Hill Cove Rd., Narragansett • Map E5*

22 Bowen's Wine Bar and Grille
9 More than 600 wines make this bar and steakhouse a wine-lover's oasis. Watch boat traffic in the harbor, while tucking into prime rib or slurping down oysters.
⬡ *22 Bowen's Wharf, Newport • Map F5*

McKinley's Waterfront
10 This warm Irish pub is a welcome find on a cool winter night, especially thanks to more than 20 ales on tap. In summer, the outdoor seating overlooking Greenwich Bay is an ideal spot to sip a brew and watch the sailboats go by. ⬡ *1 Division St., East Greenwich • Map E4*

Left **RISD Store** Center **Gray's Grist Mill** Right **Providence Place mega-mall**

Places to Shop

1 The Fantastic Umbrella Factory

No umbrellas are made here and it isn't a factory. It's a maze of unusual little shops selling work by local craftsmen and artists, novelty gifts, ethnic treasures, and even pots and plants. ◎ *4820 Old Post Rd., Charlestown • Map E5*

2 Rhode Island School of Design (RISD) Works

Creativity abounds at the shop of the RISD Museum of Art *(see p48)*, which showcases fashion, furniture, toys, and tools from alumni and faculty members. ◎ *Chace Center, 20 N. Main St., Providence • Map E4 • Closed Mon*

3 Brown & Hopkins Country Store

Children can select from the "penny candy" counter while their parents browse the home furnishings and accessories. ◎ *1179 Putnam Pike, Chepachet • Map E4*

4 Bowen's Wharf

Shops on this 18th-century wharf tend to have a nautical flavor. Landlubbers can easily outfit themselves to look like seasoned sailors. ◎ *America's Cup Ave., Newport • Map F5*

5 Warren

If it's old, you'll probably find it in Warren. A cluster of shops in the compact downtown area of this former whaling port and mill town have transformed it into a collector's paradise. ◎ *Map F4*

6 Gray's Grist Mill

For corn meal to make jonny-cakes *(see p59)* at home, stop at this old mill on a weekend to see local flint corn ground between immense stones from France. ◎ *Adamsville Rd., Adamsville • Map F5*

7 Pier Marketplace

On breaks from the beach, sunbathers browse the resort wear and gift shops of this small complex, then treat themselves to ice cream or a bag of salt-water taffy. ◎ *Narragansett Town Beach, Narragansett • Map E5*

8 Peter Pots Pottery

Collectors favor the modern lines and distinctive glazes of Peter Pots Pottery, founded in 1948. The studio, in an 18th-century mill building, displays the complete line of dinnerware and decorative pieces. ◎ *494 Glen Rock Rd., West Kingston • Map E5*

9 Providence Place

This mega-mall in the heart of downtown Providence over-looks Waterfront Park, and has every local and national chain a buyer could desire. ◎ *1 Providence Place, Providence • Map E4*

10 Garden City Center

If you prefer strolling in the outdoors, this village-like complex just 7 miles (11 km) from Providence offers the same range of shops and dining that you'll find in many enclosed malls. ◎ *Rte. 2, Cranston • Map E4*

Unless otherwise specified, shops are open daily.

Left **The old Superior Court building, New London** Right **Houseboat on Lower Connecticut River**

Connecticut

The Connecticut River – New England's largest arterial waterway – touches four states, but only gives its name to one. Settlers from Boston established Hartford on the riverbank in 1635, ultimately creating the first fully articulated constitution in the American colonies. Three years later, more Bostonians pitched their tents on Long Island Sound and created New Haven, where a small school would move in 1716 and blossom into Yale University. Harnessing the river for power, Connecticut inventors proved some of the country's most ingenious entrepreneurs. But Connecticut is as beautiful as it is industrious, as American artists demonstrated a century ago when they painted the upland woods and the spreading green and gold marshes of Long Island Sound.

First Congregational Church, Litchfield

🔟 Sights

1. Litchfield Hills
2. Hartford
3. Wethersfield
4. Gold Coast
5. New Haven
6. Midcoast Beaches
7. Lower Connecticut River
8. New London and Groton
9. Mystic and Stonington
10. Quiet Corner

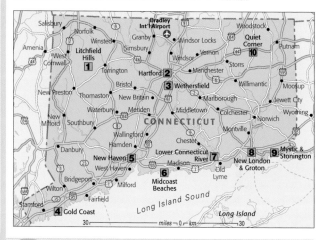

Litchfield Hills

Stretching west from the Connecticut River to the New York border, the Litchfield Hills are Connecticut's proper, manicured mountains. Model 18th- and 19th-century communities of white houses and white churches cluster around tidy town greens. In spring, waterfalls roar off the hillsides and you'll find hardy fishermen wading cold mountain brooks to cast flies for trout. In summer, the smell of newly mown lawns and the sweet scents of perennial flower gardens perfume the air (see pp18–19).

A Connecticut River-style entrance (1767), Wethersfield

Hartford

As the state capital, Hartford has a wealth of grand buildings and institutions, from the ornate Victorian-Gothic Connecticut State Capitol in Bushnell Park to America's first public art museum, the Wadsworth Atheneum (see p44), founded in 1842. Hartford was also a hotbed of 19th-century publishing and writing. The Mark Twain House (see p52), where America's greatest yarn-spinner and frontier humorist enjoyed a later life of middle-class comfort, and the charming Gothic-Revival-style Harriet Beecher Stowe Center (see p92) next door underscore the city's literary prominence.

Stop to smell the roses – more than 800 varieties of them – in Elizabeth Park, whose rose garden was created in 1904 (see p92). ◈ Map C4

Wethersfield

The epitome of Colonial and Federal style, the center of Old Wethersfield has a genteel grace that belies its early history as a frontier community beleaguered by Indian attacks. The distinctive architecture lining the community's broad streets – and the weathered headstones of its cemetery – make Old Wethersfield a destination for Colonial history buffs. ◈ Map C4

Gold Coast

The communities that lie along the stretch of the New Haven commuter rail line from Greenwich north to Norwalk are the wealthiest in Connecticut – hence the nickname "Gold Coast." When residents want to go shopping, they head to Greenwich, where boutiques cater to local hedge-fund millionaires. To dine or to party, they usually make a beeline for South Norwalk, where a bustling restaurant and bar scene has taken hold. ◈ Map B6

East Senate Chambers of Hartford's Old State House

 For more on Wethersfield See p38

New Haven

Ever since the Collegiate School moved to town in 1716, town and gown have been inextricably linked in New Haven. Fabulous collections at the Yale University Art Museums *(see p48)* and the Yale Peabody Museum of Natural History put larger cities to shame. New Haven's culinary legacy includes the legendary pizzas of Frank Pepe *(see p95),* and the hamburger – purportedly invented in 1900 at Louis' Lunch (263 Crown Street).
◈ *Map C5 • Yale Peabody Museum of Natural History: Whitney Ave. and Sachem St.; 203 432 5050; open 10am–5pm Mon–Sat, noon–5pm Sun; adm; www.yale.edu/peabody*

Tiffany stained-glass window, First Church of Christ, New Haven

Midcoast Beaches

The great shield of Long Island shelters the sandy shoreline between New Haven Harbor and the mouth of the

Bascule bridge, Mystic

Connecticut River at Old Lyme *(see p39)*. Protected from storms and erosion, the barrier beaches feature soft sand and gentle surf. Many private beach communities are located here, but so are the main state-owned beaches, including the 2-mile (3-km) strand at Hammonasset Beach State Park *(see p42)*. Communities like Branford and Clinton live for the sweet but brief summer. Shops are often seasonal. ◈ *Map C5*

Lower Connecticut River

Designated as a "last great place" by the Nature Conservancy, the lower reaches of the Connecticut, from East Haddam to Lyme, have a magical beauty that captivates artists and sustains fish and wildlife – including large numbers of bald eagles in the winter. See how the American Impressionists captured the scene at the Florence Griswold Museum *(see p92)* in Old Lyme, and explore the rich history and fascinating ecology of the region at the Connecticut River Museum in Essex. ◈ *Map D5 • Connecticut River Museum: 67 Main St., Essex; 860 767 8269; open 10am–5pm Tue–Sun (late May–early Sep daily); adm; www.ctrivermuseum.org*

New London and Groton

The deepwater port at the mouth of the Thames (pronounced to rhyme with James) River – New London on the west side, Groton on the east – lies roughly halfway between Boston and New York. It was a key base of operations for the American Navy during the Revolution; nowadays, ocean cruise ships call here. The massive shipyards

The Collegiate School, New Haven, changed its name to Yale College in 1718.

of Electric Boat, builder of nuclear-powered submarines, lie in Groton. Explore the naval legacy at the Submarine Force Museum *(see p35)*, home of the world's first nuclear-powered sub, the *USS Nautilus*. ◎ *Map D5*

Stonington village center

Mystic and Stonington
Classic small seafaring ports of the eastern Connecticut coast, Mystic and Stonington diverged when Mystic developed as a tourism center *(see pp34, 51)*. Quieter Stonington, just 4 miles (6.5 km) away, retains all the hallmarks of a 19th-century fishing and shipping port. Stonington is dotted with upscale boutiques, cheery cafés, and bars where fishermen and antiques dealers drink side by side. ◎ *Map D5, E5*

Quiet Corner
The unassuming nickname for Connecticut's northeastern corner suggests that little of excitement has happened here since General Israel Putnam killed the last wolf in Connecticut and made the region safe for sheep-farming. In truth, this area of bucolic repose is dotted with the homes of onetime country squires – including the flamboyant Roseland Cottage-Bowen House *(see p92)*. The region is often overlooked by travelers bent on reaching the Foxwoods and Mohegan Sun casinos, but antiques hunters know to stop in Putnam *(see p97)*. ◎ *Map D4*

A Walking Tour of New Haven

Morning

Start by picking up a campus map from the **Yale Visitor Center**, in the city's oldest house (1767). Then head to **City Hall** (165 Church St.), where an outdoor sculpture commemorates the *Amistad* incident. Opposite, **New Haven Green** is the site of three architecturally distinguished early-19th-century churches. Leave the green to enter Yale's **Old Campus**, with its stunning High-Victorian-Gothic buildings, through Phelps Archway on College Street. From this rarified enclave, re-enter the modern world on **Chapel Street**, where you can join students for lunch at **Claire's Corner Copia** (1000 Chapel St.), for delicious vegetarian fare.

Afternoon

After lunch, shop till you've had your fill on Chapel Street. Now explore some of Yale's innovative newer buildings, among them the **Yale Center for British Art** and the **Yale University Art Gallery** by famed modernist architect Louis Kahn. Turn right on High Street to return to the heart of campus. Across Elm Street, **Sterling Memorial Library** was built in 1930 in modern Gothic style. Yale has a wealth of public art; across from the library in Cross Campus, alumna Maya Lin's mesmerizing water sculpture honoring Yale women is a fine example. Cross Wall Street to enter Hewitt Quad, dominated by the **Beinecke Rare Book and Manuscript Library**. Follow Wall Street to a right turn onto Temple Street to return to your starting point.

Around New England – Connecticut

Treasures of the Beinecke Rare Book and Manuscript Library include a Gutenberg Bible and two volumes of Audubon's Birds of America.

Left **Lockwood-Mathews Mansion** Center **Florence Griswold Museum** Right **Glebe House**

🔟 Gardens and House Museums

1 Roseland Cottage (Bowen House)

This pink, Gothic-style cottage was the summer getaway for the wealthy New York Bowen family.
⌖ *556 Rte. 169, Woodstock • Map D4 • 860 928 4074 • Open Jun–mid Oct: Wed–Sun • Adm • www.historicnewengland.org*

2 Florence Griswold Museum

View the history of American Impressionism at this former rooming house, where artist-boarders painted more than 40 panels on the walls. ⌖ *96 Lyme St., Old Lyme • Map D5 • 860 434 5542 • Closed Mon • Adm • www.flogris.org*

3 Hill-Stead Museum

Step into an aristocratic world of privilege and elegance at this hilltop estate. ⌖ *35 Mountain Rd., Farmington • Map C4 • 860 677 4787 • Closed Mon • Adm • www.hillstead.org*

4 Elizabeth Park Rose Gardens

In June, 15,000 plants burst into bloom here, the US's oldest municipal rose garden. ⌖ *Prospect Ave., Hartford • Map C4 • Open daily • Free • www.elizabethpark.org*

5 Bush-Holley Historic Site

This museum pinpoints two revolutions in Cos Cob: the political upheaval of the 1770s and the artistic ferment of American Impressionism, 125 years later. ⌖ *39 Strickland Rd., Cos Cob • Map A6 • 203 869 6899 • Open Wed–Sun (Feb–Mar: Sat, Sun) • Adm by guided tour • www.hstg.org*

6 Glebe House Museum & Gertrude Jekyll Garden

This 1750 home has the only US garden created by famed British designer Gertrude Jekyll. ⌖ *149 Hollow Rd., Woodbury • Map B5 • 203 263 2855 • Open May–Oct: Wed–Sun; Nov: Sat, Sun • Adm • www.theglebehouse.org*

7 Lockwood-Mathews Mansion Museum

Decorative excesses abound at this estate, built for a wealthy banker and railroad tycoon. ⌖ *295 West Ave., Norwalk • Map B6 • 203 838 9799 • Open Apr–Jan: Wed–Sun • Adm • www.lockwoodmathewsmansion.com*

8 Bartlett Arboretum

Woodlands, wetlands, formal gardens, and meadows make a living museum of 850 specimen trees. ⌖ *151 Brookdale Rd., Stamford • Map A6 • 203 322 6971 • Open daily • Adm • www.bartlettarboretum.org*

9 Harriet Beecher Stowe Center

Stowe, author of *Uncle Tom's Cabin*, moved into this, her last home, in 1873. ⌖ *77 Forest St., Hartford • Map C4 • 860 522 9258 • Open Wed–Sun (Jun–Oct: Tue–Sun) • Adm • www.harrietbeecherstowecenter.org*

10 Bellamy-Ferriday House & Garden

Built for a legendary preacher in the 18th century, the final owner was a civil rights activist. ⌖ *9 Main St., Bethlehem • Map B4 • 203 266 7596 • Open May–Aug: Wed, Fri–Sun; Sep–Oct: Fri–Sun • Adm • www.ctlandmarks.org*

 For more museums See pp44–5 (art), 48–9 (university), and 52–3 (personal)

Left **Air Museum** Center **Maritime Aquarium at Norwalk** Right **Mashantucket Pequot Museum**

TOP 10 Children's Activities

1 Connecticut's Beardsley Zoo
Siberian tigers are the top cats at this 300-animal zoo. Also spy on the wolves from the observation area. ◈ *1875 Noble Ave., Bridgeport • Map B6 • 203 394 6565 • Open daily • Adm • www.beardsleyzoo.org*

2 New England Air Museum
It's hard to tell if dads or kids get more out of the 125 aircraft and 200 or so engines here. ◈ *36 Perimeter Rd., Bradley International Airport, Windsor Locks • Map C4 • 860 623 3305 • Open daily • Adm • www.neam.org*

3 Maritime Aquarium at Norwalk
This aquatic center highlights the creatures in its own backyard, like harbor seals and sleek sand tiger sharks. ◈ *10 N. Water St., Norwalk • Map B6 • 203 852 0700 • Open daily • Adm • www.maritimeaquarium.org*

4 UConn Animal Barns & Dairy Bar
Watch the cows being milked, then head to the dairy bar for freshly made farm ice cream. ◈ *University of Connecticut, Storrs • Map D4 • Animal barn: 860 486 2023 • Dairy bar: 860 486 2634 • Open daily*

5 Mashantucket Pequot Museum
This museum recounts the area's history from the perspective of its pre-colonial inhabitants. ◈ *110 Pequot Trail, Mashantucket • Map D5 • 800 411 9671 • Open Wed–Sat • Adm • www.pequotmuseum.org*

6 Ocean Beach Park
This kids' paradise features a beach, pool with waterslide, miniature golf course, and rides. ◈ *99 Neptune Ave., New London • Map D5 • 860 447 3031 • Open late May–early Sep • Adm • www.ocean-beach-park.com*

7 The Dinosaur Place
Over 25 life-sized concrete dinosaurs wait to be discovered here, along nature trails through lush woodlands. ◈ *1650 Rte. 85, Montville • Map D5 • 860 443 4367 • Park open Apr–Nov, store year-round • Adm • www.thedinosaurplace.com*

8 Essex Steam Train & Riverboat Ride
Take the throttle in a diesel-train simulator, before riding a vintage train along the Connecticut River. ◈ *1 Railroad Ave., Essex • Map D5 • 860 767 0103 or 800 377 3987 • Open May–Oct, Dec • Adm • www.essexsteamtrain.com*

9 International Skating Center of Connecticut
Many Olympic skaters train at this top ice rink which also reserves slots for public skating. ◈ *1375 Hopmeadow St., Simsbury • Map C4 • 860 651 5400 • Call for public skating hours • Adm • www.isccskate.com*

10 Garbage Museum
Learn about recycling here. The museum's mascot is a 24-ft (7.3-m) dinosaur sculpture made from discarded materials. ◈ *1410 Honeyspot Rd., Stratford • Map B6 • 203 381 9571 • Open Jul–Aug: Tue–Fri; Sep–Jun: Wed-Fri • Adm • www.crra.org*

Left **Union League Cafe** Right **Flood Tide Restaurant**

🔟 Fine Dining

Brasserie Pipp
Fine local produce and fish star in the Alsatian-style brasserie, where the chef also prepares classic French charcuterie.
🔊 *46 Main St., Ivoryton • Map D5 • 860 767 0330 • Closed L daily • $$$$*

Union League Cafe
The French chef-owner brings the hearty, market-driven cuisine of a Parisian brasserie to the sophisticated streets of New Haven near Yale University. 🔊 *1032 Chapel St., New Haven • Map C5 • 203 562 4299 • Closed Sat L, Sun • $$$$$*

Max Downtown
Tasty beef ranges from petite steak *au poivre* to giant porterhouse at this bustling urban chophouse. 🔊 *City Place, 185 Asylum St., Hartford • Map C4 • 860 522 2530 • Closed Sat & Sun L • $$$$*

Cottage Restaurant & Cafe
Years in New Orleans gave the hearty New American cooking of the chef-owner a distinct Cajun accent. Gourmet cuisine at budget prices – and her bartender brother mixes a mean cocktail. 🔊 *427 Farmington Ave., Plainville • Map C4 • 860 793 8888 • Closed Sun, Mon & Sat L • $$$*

Hopkins Inn
The menu here is laden with Austrian fare such as schnitzel and sweetbreads. The wine selection follows suit. 🔊 *22 Hopkins Rd., New Preston • Map B4 • 860 868 7295 • Open B, L, D Tue–Sun (Tue–Sat Jan–late Mar) • $$$$*

Restaurant Jean-Louis
Connecticut's most acclaimed chef has perfected a light version of classical French cuisine. The intimate dining room makes for a romantic setting. 🔊 *61 Lewis St., Greenwich • Map A6 • 203 622 8450 • Closed Sat L, Sun • $$$$$*

Good News Cafe
The chef-owner insists on using only local, sustainable, organic products. But her food is never precious, just delicious. 🔊 *694 Main St. S., Woodbury • Map B5 • 203 266 4663 • Closed Tue • $$$$*

Match
Sparkling seafood dishes, inventive seasonal American fare, and rich desserts are a perfect match to the hippest bar on SoNo's restaurant row. 🔊 *98 Washington St., South Norwalk • Map B6 • 203 852 1088 • Closed L • $$$$*

Flood Tide Restaurant
Views of Long Island Sound and the ambience of soft piano music are a great match for the market-led cuisine. Diners near the open kitchen can watch chefs play with fire. 🔊 *Inn at Mystic, 3 Williams Ave., Mystic • Map D5 • 860 536 9604 or 800 237 2415 • Closed L • $$$*

85 Main
Sample the superb seafood in either the cozy dining room or the blue-and-white tiled bar. 🔊 *85 Main St., Putnam • Map D4 • 860 928 1660 • $$$$*

All restaurants open for lunch and dinner daily unless indicated. Most require reservations to avoid long waits.

Price Categories

For a three course meal for one with half a bottle of wine (or equivalent meal), taxes and extra charges.

\$	under \$25
\$\$	\$25–\$40
\$\$\$	\$40–\$50
\$\$\$\$	\$50–\$65
\$\$\$\$\$	over \$65

Left **Frank Pepe Pizzeria Napoletana** Right **Mystic Pizza**

🔟 Casual Dining

1 Frank Pepe Pizzeria Napoletana

The thin-crust pizza at this no-frills joint open since 1925 has an almost cult following among Yale students. White clam pizza (no tomato sauce) is among the most popular. ◈ *157 Wooster St., New Haven • Map C5 • 203 865 5762 • \$*

2 O'Rourke's Diner

Dating from the mid-1940s, the best food at this classic diner comes fresh off the grill. ◈ *728 Main St., Middletown • Map C5 • 860 346 6101 • Open 5am–2pm Sun–Thu, 5am–9pm Fri–Sat • \$*

3 Rawley's Drive-In

When customers stand in line for 20 minutes, it's clear a restaurant is doing something right. At Rawley's, it's the hot dogs that keep them coming back for more. ◈ *1886 Post Rd., Rte. 1, Fairfield • Map B6 • 203 259 9023 • Open 11am–6:30pm Mon–Sat • \$*

4 The Cookhouse

Wood-smoked barbecued meat is nearly a religion here. Top sellers are pork back ribs, Carolina-style pulled pork, and slow-roasted beef brisket. ◈ *31 Danbury Rd., New Milford • Map B5 • 860 355 4111 • \$*

5 Blackie's Hot Dog Stand

Since 1928, Blackie's has offered hot dogs with or without homemade spicy pepper relish, birch beer on tap, and chocolate milk. ◈ *2200 Waterbury Rd., Cheshire • Map C5 • 203 699 1819 • Closed Fri • \$*

6 Mystic Pizza

A Julia Roberts movie made this pizza-and-pasta joint famous, but diners keep returning for the excellent "secret recipe" tomato sauce that's generously slathered on the pizzas. ◈ *56 W Main St., Mystic • Map D5 • 860 536 3700 • \$*

7 Shady Glen

The homemade ice cream is great, but it's the cheeseburgers that are the top stars here. ◈ *840 E. Middle Tpk., Manchester • Map C4 • 860 649 4245 • Open B, L, D daily • \$*

8 Cove Fresh Fish Market

Clam fritters, whole-belly fried clams, and the fried cod sandwich are the most popular plates at Cove, a seafood market that also cooks the catch. ◈ *20 Old Stonington Rd., Mystic • Map D5 • 860 536 0061 • Open Jun–Sep: 11am–8pm Mon–Thu, Sun, 11am–9pm Fri–Sat; Oct–May: 11am–7.30pm Wed–Sun • \$*

9 Rein's

Who'd have thought that central Connecticut would make better Jewish deli food than most of New York? Chopped liver, latkes ... It's a quick stop off highway I-84. ◈ *435 Hartford Tpk., Vernon • Map C4 • 860 875 1344 • \$*

10 West Street Grill

Casual lunches are a big hit here, especially the burgers and the pulled short-rib beef sandwich. Strong New American dinner menu. ◈ *43 West St., Litchfield • Map B4 • 860 567 3885 • \$\$\$\$*

Casual eating spots like these may cut back hours outside summer season. Call to check.

Left **Toad's Place** Right **Water Street Cafe**

Cafés and Bars

The Loft
Connecticut's best martinis are all you really need to know about The Loft, so named for the people-watching mezzanine up a wrought iron staircase. ✆ *97 Washington St., S. Norwalk • Map B6*

Black-Eyed Sally's
Blues and barbecue grew up together in the Mississippi Delta, and Sally's serves up both. The Southern juke-joint ambience matches the musicians that perform here. ✆ *350 Asylum St., Hartford • Map C4*

Toad's Place
One of the state's biggest dance floors and a sound system that could rock a stadium make Toad's *the* dance venue on a Saturday night. ✆ *300 York St., New Haven • Map C5*

Pastorale Bistro & Bar
Lauded for its French bistro classics made with locally grown ingredients, this bistro and *boîte* in a 1760 Colonial house boasts a sophisticated list of cocktails and a good wine cellar. ✆ *223 Main St., Salisbury • Map B4 • www.pastorale bistro.com*

Water Street Cafe
Locals favor Water Street for great oysters at the raw bar, chilled white wine, and live guitar music, but don't overlook lively dishes like the lobster spring rolls or warm duck salad. ✆ *143 Water St., Stonington • Map E5*

@ The Corner
This hip bakery (formerly The Blue Bakery) makes frosting-piled cakes and pies bursting with fillings. It also serves good coffee and espresso, and a selection of soups, sandwiches, and salads. ✆ *3 West St., Litchfield • Map B4*

MacDuff's Public House
There's a certain amount of tartan posturing in the decor of this upscale Scottish-themed pub. European soccer often dominates the TV over the bar. ✆ *99 Railroad Ave., Greenwich • Map A6*

Max's Oyster Bar
Showmanlike presentation of the raw-bar offerings sets the tone for this polished, dressy seafood restaurant. ✆ *964 Farmington Ave., West Hartford • Map C4 • 860 236 6299 • Closed Sun L; open Sun brunch • www.maxrestaurantgroup.com*

Delaney's Tap Room
Beer is taken seriously here, with 60 active taps going at a time. Another 120 beers come in bottles. The bartenders are winners of the national Stella Artois beer-pouring contest. ✆ *882 Whalley Ave., New Haven • Map C5*

Wine Bar at the Griswold Inn
Mature cheeses and tapas-style platters can be matched with at least 50 wines at this intimate bar, where the walls are covered with maritime art. ✆ *36 Main St., Essex • Map D5*

Around New England – Connecticut

Left **Olde Mistick Village** Center **Ceramics, Guilford Art Center** Right **Woodbury Pewter**

🔟 Places to Shop

1 "The Avenue," Greenwich
Greenwich is the "platinum" town on Connecticut's Gold Coast, and Greenwich Avenue is packed with luxury boutiques to feather the finest nest. ✎ *Map A6*

2 Guilford Art Center
The town green bustles each July with a juried exhibition of fine crafts. But this center promotes crafts year-round, with classes and a shop full of unique hand-crafted items. ✎ *411 Church St., Guilford • Map C5*

3 The Shops at Mohegan Sun
Visitors who strike it rich at the gaming tables and slot machines will find plenty to tempt them in the upscale shops of this casino complex. ✎ *1 Mohegan Sun Blvd., Uncasville • Map D5*

4 Woodbury Pewter
You might find the perfect candlestick, bowl, or teapot at a discount at the factory outlet of this family-owned company, founded in 1952. ✎ *860 Main St. S., Woodbury • Map B5*

5 Stamford
Interior decorators scour the immense United House Wrecking for architectural salvage, lawn ornaments, or unusual furniture and accessories. If you're not driving a van, other shops in town stock smaller collectibles. ✎ *United House Wrecking: 535 Hope St., Stamford • Map A6*

6 Olde Mistick Village
Lush gardens, a duck pond, and a waterwheel accent this quaint complex not far from Mystic Seaport *(see p34)*. There's even an old-fashioned general store. ✎ *Coogan Blvd., Mystic • Map D5*

7 The Silo Store
Musician Skitch Henderson and his wife left their farm to a trust. The couple loved fine food; the shop (in the farm's silo) features gourmet cookware and hosts cooking classes. ✎ *44 Upland Rd., New Milford • Map B5*

8 Chapel St., New Haven
Chapel Street skirts the edge of the Yale campus with shops catering to the whims of faculty and students alike. Look for a retro head shop, designer clothing boutiques, and book-store cafés. ✎ *Map C5*

9 Putnam
Setting up the Antiques Marketplace in an ex-department store breathed new life into this former mill town. If you can't find your collectible there, check the town's smaller shops. ✎ *Antiques Marketplace: 109 Main St. • Map D4*

10 Clinton Crossing Premium Outlets
Get a "champagne" wardrobe on a "plonk" budget. Stores include DKNY, Calvin Klein, Kenneth Cole, and outlets for Saks Fifth Avenue and Barneys New York. ✎ *20-A Killingworth Tpke., Clinton • Map C5*

Left **Green Mountain National Forest** Right **Restored house in Woodstock village**

Vermont

Things are always looking up in Vermont – unless you're looking down from the top of a ski run. The majestic Green Mountains that cover the state compensate for the lack of a seacoast. Between the peaks stand high green meadows and deep, dark lakes, two of which are said to harbor sea serpents. Settled in the 1700s under conflicting land grants from New York and New Hampshire, Vermont was an independent republic from 1777, becoming the 14th US state in 1791. A rugged independence persists in Vermonters, who despite severe winter weather seem to be outdoors year-round – hiking, skiing, skating, sledding, cycling, kayaking, hunting, and fishing. If you wanted a single image to sum up Vermont, you could do worse than a four-wheel-drive vehicle with a bike rack on top emerging from one of the state's 107 covered bridges against a brilliant background of autumn leaves.

Angler on Lake Quechee

🔟 Sights

1. Green Mountains
2. Brattleboro
3. Grafton
4. Woodstock and Quechee
5. Montpelier
6. Shelburne
7. Burlington
8. Northeast Kingdom
9. Newport
10. St. Johnsbury

Green Mountains

It would scarcely be an exaggeration to say that Vermont *is* the Green Mountains and vice versa, as this ancient range in the Appalachian chain touches almost every part of the state *(see pp20–21)*.

Brattleboro

Vermont's first permanent English settlement, Brattleboro flourished in the 19th century as a Connecticut River manufacturing town at the juncture of Vermont, New Hampshire, and Massachusetts. The town got a new lease on life in the 1960s as the counterculture capital of the upper Connecticut River Valley, and is known around the state for its stridently liberal politics. The thriving cultural community includes several galleries, a performing arts center, and a school of circus arts which is open to the general public. ✪ Map K6

Grafton

Wealthy philanthropists saved this beautiful village in the 1960s when they formed the Windham Foundation to restore its handsome historic buildings and revitalize commerce. They did a great job. Stop to visit Plummer's Sugar House, sample the excellent cheddars of the Grafton Village Cheese Co., or refresh yourself at The Old Tavern, a 200-year-old inn and restaurant that functions as the de facto local tourist office.

✪ *Map K6 • Plummer's Sugar House: 123 Townshend Rd.; 802 843 2207; www.plummers sugarhouse.com • Grafton Village Cheese Co.: 533 Townshend Rd.; 800 472 3866; www.grafton villagecheese.com • Old Tavern: 92 Main St.; 802 843 2231*

Grafton mailbox

Woodstock and Quechee

It's little wonder that Woodstock is such a popular destination for weddings and civil unions. With its broad town green, meticulously restored Federal and Victorian houses, covered bridge in the middle of town, and five churches boasting Paul Revere bells, it is the very picture of old-time Vermont. Even the Billings Farm *(see p32)* serves as a museum of Vermont rural life. Head east on Route 4 to see the vertigo-inspiring 165-ft (50-m) deep gorge carved by the Ottauquechee River. ✪ Map K5

Vermont State House, Montpelier

Montpelier

For an iconic Vermont image, stop along State Street during foliage season to take a snapshot of the gold-domed State House backed by a hillside of red and flame-orange maple trees. The city was selected for state capital in 1805 because it lies at the geographic center of Vermont as well as in the main east-west pass through the Green Mountains. The highly regarded New England Culinary Institute guarantees that Montpelier eats well, especially at the school's NECI on Main *(see p105)*. ✪ Map K3

Ethan Allen

Vermont folk hero Ethan Allen (1738–89) led a militia called the Green Mountain Boys. He is hailed for rebuffing colonial governors and British troops alike in a quest for Vermont's independence. His capture of Fort Ticonderoga from British forces in 1775 played a key strategic role early in the American Revolution.

Boats docked at Lake Champlain, Burlington

Shelburne

6 Standing on high banks above Lake Champlain just south of Burlington, Shelburne is a village of magnificent dairy farms, not least among them the historic spread of Shelburne Farms (see p103). A locomotive, a steamship, and buildings crammed with folk art dot the rolling meadows of Shelburne Museum (see p45). South of town, just into Charlotte, the Vermont Wildflower Farm has over 350 species of flowering plants and trees on the grounds. Get seeds at the farm shop.
Ⓝ Map J3 • Vermont Wildflower Farm: 3488 Ethan Allen Hwy., Charlotte; 802 425 3641; open Apr–Oct: 10am–5pm daily; free; www.vermontwildflowerfarm.com

Burlington

7 Settled shortly before the American Revolution, Burlington, unlike the rest of Vermont, takes

Shelburne village center

its identity less from the Green Mountains than from the great inland sea of Lake Champlain. Burlington shipyards turned the mountain timber into trading vessels. Learn about the city's boating history at the Lake Champlain Maritime Museum (see p35). Blessed with a handsome, largely 19th-century downtown, Burlington also enjoys a busy cultural life as a by-product of the presence of the state university. Ⓝ Map J3

Northeast Kingdom

8 "Northeast Kingdom" refers to Essex, Orleans, and Caledonia counties in the state's northeast corner – an area sometimes referred to simply as "The Kingdom". In Vermont cultural shorthand, the term connotes both a rural, frontier toughness and an easy familiarity with the latest developments in the world of avant-garde performance art. With only two large communities – St. Johnsbury and Newport – it is one of the most rural parts of the state. The Northeast Kingdom is known above all for skiing, resplendent autumn foliage, and delicious maple syrup. Ⓝ Map L2

Newport

9 Vermont's northernmost city sits at the southern edge of Lake Memphremagog, a body of water 27 miles (43 km) long

that is shared with the province of Quebec. A glacial lake that was a saltwater inland sea at the end of the Laurentian glaciation, Memphremagog has long been rumored to hold a sea serpent akin to the Loch Ness Monster. Sightings of the elusive creature that locals call "Memphre" date to the 18th century. Take a stroll along the attractive waterfront and see if you can spy those watery coils from the safety of the shore. ◈ Map L5

St. Johnsbury Athenaeum Art Gallery

St. Johnsbury

"St. J," as Vermonters call it, is both the hub of the state's Northeast Kingdom and the gateway between the Green Mountains of Vermont and the White Mountains of New Hampshire. When Thaddeus Fairbanks invented the platform scale in 1830, St. Johnsbury was his manufacturing center. The Fairbanks clan left its stamp on the town, donating both the Fairbanks Museum & Planetarium *(see p102)*, and the Athenaeum, a library and gallery with magnificent landscape paintings. ◈ Map L3 • *Athenaeum Gallery: 1171 Main St.; 802 748 8291; open 10am–5:30pm Mon–Fri, 9:30am–5pm Sat (to 3pm in summer); adm; www.stjathenaeum.org*

A Day Hiking in Robert Frost Country

Morning

Robert Frost (1874–1963), the seminal poet of the New England countryside, spent 39 summers in the Green Mountain National Forest. This easy-to-moderate day of hiking captures the poet and the landscape he loved. Start with pancakes and maple syrup at the **Rochester Cafe** (Rte. 100, Rochester; 802 767 4302), at the same soda fountain where Frost used to eat, and have the café pack you a lunch. Drive west on Rte. 125 to the **Robert Frost Interpretive Trail**, where you can read some of Frost's pithy verse and learn to identify native plants. Just east of the almost adjacent Robert Frost Wayside picnic area, a 5-minute walk on an unmarked dirt road will bring you to Frost's cabin at the **Homer Noble Farm**, maintained as he left it.

Afternoon

When the muse evaded Frost, he sought solace in the woods. For a hike (rather than a stroll), head east on Rte. 125 a short distance and turn left onto **Steam Mill Road**. A little way further on, park at the **Skylight Pond** trailhead. The well-blazed path ascends the flank of Battell Mountain, crisscrossing the hillside through a forest of white birch, red oak, and hemlocks. Overgrown and tumbledown stone walls proclaim old boundary lines, as forest reclaims farmland. The moderate 45-minute climb ends on a ridge connecting to the legendary Long Trail. Turn left for a short hike to **Skyline Lodge**, a rustic shelter for hikers.

Left **Institute of Natural Science** Center **UVM Morgan Horse Farm** Right **Vermont Ski Museum**

Best of the Rest

1 President Calvin Coolidge State Historic Site

The independent spirit of his home village inspired Coolidge (1872–1933). Today, he would still recognize many sites. ✪ 3780 Rte. 100 A, Plymouth • Map K5 • 802 672 3773 • Open daily late May–mid-Oct • Adm • www.historicvermont.org

2 Fairbanks Museum & Planetarium

Vermont flora and fauna mingle with Philippine and Indian birds in this natural history museum. ✪ 1302 Main St., St. Johnsbury • Map L3 • 802 748 2372 • Closed Mon Nov–Mar • Adm • www.fairbanksmuseum.org

3 UVM Morgan Horse Farm

The graceful Morgan horse, one of the first US breeds, is bred here. ✪ 74 Battell Dr., Weybridge • Map J4 • 802 388 2011 • Open daily May–Oct • Adm • www.uvm.edu/morgan

4 Bennington Museum & Grandma Moses Gallery

Stop by and browse this major collection of work by folk artist Grandma Moses (1860–1961). ✪ 75 Main St., Bennington • Map J6 • 802 447 1571 • Closed Jan; Wed • Adm • www.benningtonmuseum.org

5 Vermont Ski Museum

Skis, chairlifts, and gondolas chart skiing in Vermont from the introduction of powered lifts in the 1930s to the present day. ✪ 1 S. Main St., Stowe • Map K3 • 802 253 9911 • Closed Tue, Nov, Apr–May • donation • www.vermontskimuseum.org

6 Robert Hull Fleming Museum

Artifacts ranging from African masks and pre-Columbian pottery to medieval manuscripts and Andy Warhol prints are displayed here. ✪ 61 Colchester Ave., Burlington • Map J3 • 802 656 2090 • Closed Mon; mid-Dec–mid-Jan; mid-Mar • Adm • www.uvm.edu/~fleming

7 Vermont Institute of Natural Science

Injured eagles, hawks, and other raptors, unable to return to the wild, get a second home here. ✪ 6565 Woodstock Rd., Rte. 4, Quechee • Map K5 • 802 359 5000 • Adm • www.vinsweb.org

8 Montshire Museum

Nature trails at this science museum amplify the natural history exhibits. ✪ 1 Montshire Rd., Norwich • Map L4 • 802 649 2200 • Open daily • Adm • www.montshire.org

9 Vermont Covered Bridge Museum

Learn how Vermont's iconic bridges were constructed. ✪ Rte. 9 at Gypsy Ln., Bennington • Map J6 • 802 442 7158 • Closed Tue May–Dec, Sun Jan–Apr • Adm • www.benningtoncenterforthearts.org

10 American Museum of Fly Fishing

Rods, reels, flies, and books tell the story of this most philosophical of outdoor pursuits. ✪ 4104 Main St., Manchester • Map K6 • 802 362 3300 • Closed Mon May–Oct, Sun–Mon Nov–Apr • Adm • www.amff.com

Left **Cold Hollow Cider Mill** Center **Ben & Jerry's** Right **Shelburne Farms**

⟨10⟩ Tastes of Vermont

1 Cold Hollow Cider Mill
Drop by for the zing of freshly-pressed cider. The store brims with Vermont specialties. ◈ *3600 Waterbury-Stowe Rd., Rte. 100, Waterbury Center • Map K3 • 802 244 8771 • Open daily • Free • www. coldhollow.com*

2 Lake Champlain Chocolates
See local cream and butter blended with fine chocolate to form decadent bars and truffles. ◈ *750 Pine St., Burlington • Map J3 • 802 864 1808 • Factory tours: Mon–Fri • Free • www.lakechamplainchocolates.com*

3 Magic Hat Brewery
Magic Hat's oddball brews include raspberry stout, honey ale, and bourbon-cask-aged lager. ◈ *5 Bartlett Bay Rd., S. Burlington • Map J3 • 802 658 2739 • Open daily • Free • www.magichat.net*

4 Ben & Jerry's Ice Cream Factory
Vermont farms provide the rich milk for the super-premium ice creams and yogurts. ◈ *Rte. 100, Waterbury • Map K3 • 866 BJ TOURS • Open daily • Adm • www.benjerry.com*

5 Maple Grove Farms Maple Museum and Gift Shop
Learn how tree sap becomes a breakfast favorite. Then watch that maple syrup further transformed into candies. ◈ *1052 Portland St., St. Johnsbury • Map L3 • 802 748 5141 • Open Apr–May: Mon–Fri; Jun–Dec: daily • Adm • www.maplegrove.com*

6 Bragg Farm Sugar House & Gift Shop
On weekends in March and April, enjoy the local specialty "sugar on snow." In summer, cool off with a maple milkshake at this family operation. ◈ *Rte. 14 N., E. Montpelier • Map K3 • 802 223 5757 • Open daily • www.braggfarm.com*

7 Shelburne Farms
Watch milk from Brown Swiss cows turned into superb cheddar at this farm overlooking Lake Champlain. ◈ *1611 Harbor Rd., Shelburne • Map J3 • 802 985 8442 • Store open daily; tours May–Oct • Adm for tours • www.shelburnefarms.org*

8 Cabot Creamery
The shop at Vermont's largest cheese producer stocks a wide range of dairy products, from aged cheddars to rich butters and yogurt. ◈ *2878 Main St., Cabot • Map L3 • 800 837 4261 • Closed Sun Nov–May • Adm (for tour) • www.cabotcheese.com*

9 Crowley Cheese Co.
This is Vermont's oldest cheese factory (1882), noted for its prize-winning Colby cheese. ◈ *14 Crowley Ln., Healdville • Map K5 • 802 259 2340 • Open Mon–Sat • www. crowleycheese-vermont.com*

10 Vermont Country Store
This emporium still has a pickle barrel and huge wedges of cheddar. Try its own Vermont Common Crackers. ◈ *657 Main St., Weston • Map K5 • 802 824 3184 • Open daily • www.vermontcountrystore.com*

Left **Shed Restaurant and Brewery** Right **Perfect Wife Tavern**

Top 10 Bars and Cafés

1 Shed Restaurant and Brewery
Take your pick of the quiet dining room or boisterous pub for a menu strong on hearty burgers, barbecued ribs, and the like. The on-site brewery makes excellent English-style ales. ◎ *1859 Mountain Rd., Stowe • Map K3 • 802 253 4364 • $$*

2 The Alchemist Pub and Brewery
The eclectic menu at this art-filled pub emphasizes burgers, burritos, and pizzettas. Wash it all down with beer from the basement brewery. ◎ *23 S. Main St., Waterbury • Map K3 • $*

3 McGrath's Irish Pub
Darts, Guinness on draft, and live music on weekends await you at this amiable pub. ◎ *Inn at Long Trail, 709 Rte. 4, Sherburne Pass, Killington • Map K5*

4 Baba-a-Louis Bakery
In addition to selling French baguettes and organic whole wheat loaves to take home, there's a lunch buffet featuring sandwiches and soups. ◎ *92 Rte. 11 W., Chester • Map K5*

5 Drink
This sophisticated northern Vermont bar offers splashy mojitos, cosmopolitans, and a selection of home-infused vodkas. Traditionalists may bypass the lounge in favor of beer and televised sports at the bar. ◎ *135 St. Paul St., Burlington • Map J3*

6 Bentley's Restaurant
The overstuffed sofas, oriental carpets, and antique lamps might remind you of your aunt's Victorian parlor, but Bentley's is a lively spot for a hearty meal, custom-brewed ale, and weekend dancing. ◎ *3 Elm St., Woodstock • Map K5 • 802 457 3232 • $$*

7 Jasper Murdock's Alehouse
This cozy Norwich pub brews its own English-style ales. It attracts large numbers of students from nearby Dartmouth College, as well as local ski buffs. ◎ *325 Main St., Norwich • Map L4*

8 Matterhorn
The first bar south of Stowe's Mt. Mansfield, the Matterhorn is party central after a day of skiing. Duck into the sophisticated martini bar to escape the hubbub. ◎ *4969 Mountain Rd., Stowe • Map K3*

9 Perfect Wife Tavern
Judging by the menu, a "perfect wife" can cook a pot of chili or grill a steelhead trout. Live music on weekends brings in the local crowd. ◎ *2594 Depot St., Manchester Center • Map K6 • $*

10 Mocha Joe's Cafe
Artists, musicians, and all self-respecting Brattleboro Bohemians get caffeinated at this roaster café known for its winter maple lattes and summer limeade. ◎ *82 Main St., Brattleboro • Map K6*

Left **The Farmers Diner** Right **Simon Pearce Restaurant**

Price Categories

For a three course meal for one with half a bottle of wine (or equivalent meal), taxes and extra charges.	**$** under $25
	$$ $25–$40
	$$$ $40–$50
	$$$$ $50–$65
	$$$$$ over $65

⑩ Restaurants

1 Inn at Shelburne Farms Restaurant
This elegant dining room makes the most of northern Vermont's short but high-grade harvest, from early lettuces to fall apples. ⊘ *1611 Harbor Rd., Shelburne • Map J3 • 802 985 8498 • Open mid-May–mid-Oct, B and D daily, Sun brunch • $$$$*

2 The Belted Cow Bistro
Champions of farm-to-fork dining, the talented chef-owners Caitlin and John serve up the contemporary flavors of Vermont. ⊘ *4 Park Way, Essex Junction • Map J3 • 802 316 3883 • Closed L, Sun–Mon • $$$$*

3 NECI on Main
Student chefs at the New England Culinary Institute start their training here. Weekend brunch features stunning European charcuterie. ⊘ *118 Main St., Montpelier • Map K3 • 802 223 3188 • Closed Mon; open Sat & Sun brunch • $$*

4 The Farmers Diner
The focus at this Quechee Gorge diner is on top-grade local produce. ⊘ *5573 Woodstock Rd., Rte. 4, Quechee • Map K5 • 802 295 4600 • Open B & L daily • $*

5 Simon Pearce Restaurant
Savor the scenic riverside location, superb food, and fine wine. Pearce, a famed glass artist, has a studio on site. ⊘ *1760 Quechee Main St., Quechee • Map K5 • 802 295 1470 • Closed Sun L; open Sun brunch • $$$*

6 Kitchen Table Bistro
This cozy bistro operated by two graduates of the New England Culinary Institute has a strong northern-French accent. Try the maple-smoked pork and braised kale. ⊘ *1840 W. Main St., Richmond • Map K3 • 802 434 8686 • Closed L, Sun & Mon D • $$$$*

7 Starry Night Café
Dining here in a covered bridge or a former cider house is as magical as the restaurant name. The hearty American food is mostly raised or grown locally. ⊘ *5371 Rte. 7, Ferrisburg • Map J3 • 802 877 6316 • Closed L, Mon & Tue D • $$$$*

8 Hemingway's
This celebrated romantic restaurant excels at healthful New American cuisine with superb wines. ⊘ *4988 Rte. 4, Killington • Map K5 • 802 422 3886 • Closed L, Mon; Tue in summer • $$$$$*

9 The Inn at Sawmill Farm
If you didn't know that the lamb, pheasant, and venison are all Vermont-reared, you'd swear you were in a starred Burgundy restaurant. ⊘ *7 Crosstown Rd., West Dover • Map K6 • 802 464 8131 • Closed L; open B daily (inn guests only) • $$$$*

10 The Inn at Weathersfield
The inventive chef here might pair pork loin and scallops with capers, or pumpkin soup with local blue cheese. ⊘ *1342 Rte. 106, Perkinsville • Map K5 • 802 263 9217 • Closed L, Mon–Wed D • $$$$*

All restaurants open for lunch and dinner daily unless indicated.

Left **Hood Museum of Art, Hanover** Right **Tugs on the Piscataqua River, Portsmouth**

New Hampshire

The aptly nicknamed Granite State is a thick wedge of rock between two great rivers – the Connecticut on the west and the Piscataqua on the east. Its initial settlements in the 1620s were strictly coastal, but within a generation, explorers had ventured deep into its woods for furs and timber, and despite the rugged topography, many of the villages in the White Mountains were well underway by the time of the American Revolution. Most residents live along the southern edge of the state, often driving to Massachusetts for employment. Northern New Hampshire remains almost untracked forest. American scenic tourism began in the White Mountains in the 1820s, and those peaks and the villages on their flanks remain major vacation destinations. New Hampshire also boasts a chain of alpine lakes and a short but lively seacoast, where vacationers from as far away as Montreal flock to the shore.

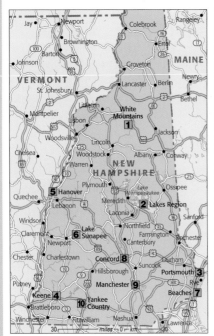

Chocorua Lake in New Hampshire's Lakes Region

🔟 Sights

1. White Mountains
2. Lakes Region
3. Portsmouth
4. Keene
5. Hanover
6. Lake Sunapee
7. Beaches
8. Concord
9. Manchester
10. Yankee Country

Preceding pages **Winter in Vermont**

1 White Mountains

The White Mountains have a special place in American history. When early-19th-century poets, philosophers, and theologians sought inspiration, they made a pilgrimage to these majestic hills to experience the sublime (see pp16–17).

White Mountains

2 Lakes Region

Vast lakes and small ponds form a watery belt across New Hampshire's midriff. Seek solitude among the loons on a remote cove, or party all night on Weirs Beach (see pp24–5).

3 Portsmouth

Portsmouth was New Hampshire's first English community, settled at the mouth of the Piscataqua River in 1623. Plentiful timber and a deep harbor made it a natural for ship-building, and from 1780 to 1870 its merchant traders grew rich. Walk the handsome squares of the Colonial settlement to see some of New England's finest in-town mansions – and to breathe the salt air that has always been Portsmouth's life-blood. The historic houses of Strawbery Banke (see p32) relate the city's four-century domestic history. ◎ Map N6

Central square, Keene

4 Keene

At 132 ft (40 m) wide for most of its length, Keene's Main Street is easily the widest in New England – wide enough to absorb the tens of thousands who come to town for the annual Pumpkin Festival (see p65). Keene regularly lights 20,000-plus jack-o'-lanterns in the finale. For the rest of the year it's a more sober-minded shire town with a lively mix of shops and art galleries, and the good bars and cafés you'd expect in a college community. ◎ Map L6

5 Hanover

It's hardly a bad thing, but Dartmouth College utterly overwhelms the rest of Hanover. The town green and the college green are one and the same, and the shopping district clearly favors the tastes of young scholars and their well-heeled parents. But Dartmouth holds many riches, even for the visitor just passing through. Not least among them are the art treasures of the Hood Museum (see p49). Most recreational programs of the Dartmouth Outing Club, including boat rentals, are open to non-students as well. ◎ Map L4
• Ledyard Canoe Club of D.O.C.: Ledyard Bridge; 603 643 6709; open daily mid-May–Sep; adm

Lake Sunapee

This alpine lake – its name, meaning "wild goose waters," is of American-Indian origin – was a major Victorian resort where vacationers stepped off the train onto steamboats to be delivered to their grand lakefront hotels. The hotels are gone, but private cottages (many for rent) ring the lake, and the harbors of Sunapee and Newbury are busy spots in the summer, with free outdoor concerts and bustling restaurants. Tour the lake on steamboat replica *MV Kearsarge*. Map L5 • MV Kearsage: Lake Ave., Sunapee; 603 938 6465; open late May–mid-Oct; adm; www.mvkearsarge.com

Boats on Lake Sunapee

Beaches

New Hampshire's brief stretch of coastline is more rock than sand, with rugged promontories and rock jetties protecting its fishing harbors. The coast is also punctuated by swathes of coarse brown sand. Jenness State Beach and Wallis Sands State Beach in Rye and North Beach in Hampton have the best-maintained facilities and gentlest swimming. Hampton Beach (see p42) is by far the most popular. Map N6

Museum of New Hampshire History, Concord

Concord

The state capital, Concord is a serene little town steeped in history. Its handsome 1819 State House is one of the country's oldest. The celebrated Concord stagecoaches that helped to open up the American West were manufactured here; Mark Twain memorably described one as being "like a cradle on wheels." The city's most famous modern resident was schoolteacher Christa McAuliffe (1948–86), who died aboard the *Challenger* space shuttle. Her dedication to science education is memorialized at the McAuliffe-Shepard Discovery Center (see p50). Map M5 • Museum of New Hampshire History: 6 Eagle Sq.; 603 228 6688; open 9:30am–5pm Tue–Sat, noon–5pm Sun (also 9:30am–5pm Mon Jul–mid-Oct and Dec); adm; www.nhhistory.org

Mt. Monadnock, from Gilson Pond, Jaffrey

Manchester

The largest city in northern New England, Manchester rose and fell with the Amoskeag Mill. From humble beginnings in 1809 on the east bank of the Merrimack River, it grew into the world's largest cotton-mill complex by the dawn of the 20th century. The textile era has long since ended in Manchester, but the hulking brick mills have been transformed into a lively complex of restaurants, college classrooms, offices, and apartments. The city's comprehensive Currier Museum of Art *(see p44)* is the state's premier art museum. ◈ Map M6

Yankee Country

It's no surprise that Yankee Publishing, which produces both *Yankee Magazine* and the *Old Farmer's Almanac*, is based in the rural village of Dublin. The homespun village and its neighboring towns of Jaffrey and Peterborough epitomize the gentle New England countryside. The region was a popular resort area in the late 19th century, and all three villages have long served as staging grounds for people preparing to climb nearby Mount Monadnock *(see p37)* – if local lore is to be believed, the second most-climbed peak in the world after Japan's Mount Fuji. ◈ Map L6

A Day's Drive on the Kancamagus Highway

Morning

Before you begin the 35-mile (56-km) drive from Lincoln to Conway, stop at **Half Baked & Fully Brewed** (187 Main St., Lincoln) for picnic fixings. After a gentle 11-mile (18-km) rise, you'll climb steeply through switchbacks for 4 miles (6 km) to the **Graham Wangan Ground Overlook** for jaw-dropping mountain views. As the road twists and turns for another 6 miles (10 km), watch for a right turn into the trailhead to **Sabbaday Falls**. A short walk through dense, pine-scented woods brings you to the waterfall, which makes a dramatic 90-degree dog-leg as it tumbles down a mountain. The **Rocky Gorge Scenic Area**, a further 4 miles (6 km) east, is a geological wonder. Cross a bridge to follow a short trail to **Falls Pond**, where fishermen cast for trout.

Afternoon

Another 3 miles (5 km) east, spread your food on a picnic table at **Lower Falls**, overlooking the boulder-strewn **Swift River**. The green pools below the largest boulders make cool summer swimming holes. In the fall, photographers scramble across the boulders trying to capture the intense red and yellow foliage. From the Falls, it's only a short drive to the Albany covered bridge *(see p37)*. The weathered 120-foot (37-m) span is a favorite with photographers and you'll surely want a shot to remember your journey. From the bridge, it's about 7 fairly flat miles (11 km) to the end of the "Kanc" in Conway.

The Kancamagus Highway (see p36) is most popular with leaf-peepers, but the twisting road makes an exhilarating drive any time.

Left **Enfield Shaker Museum** Center **Crawford Notch** Right **Pershing Tank, Wright Museum**

TOP 10 Best of the Rest

1 Odiorne Point State Park
Tidal pools, pebble beaches, and marshlands surround the site of New Hampshire's first English settlement. ⊛ *Rte. 1A, Rye • Map N6 • 603 436 7406 • Open late May–early Sep: daily • Adm • www.nhstateparks.org*

2 Mount Kearsarge Indian Museum
Admire intricate craftwork and learn how plants were used for food and medicine. ⊛ *Kearsarge Mountain Rd., Warner • Map L5 • 603 456 2600 • Closed Jan–Apr, Nov–Dec Mon–Fri • Adm • www.indianmuseum.org*

3 Mount Sunapee State Park
There's a pristine lake for swimming, fishing, and boating, as well as 65 ski trails in winter. ⊛ *Rte. 103, Newbury • Map L5 • 603 763 5561 (park); 603 763 3500 (resort) • Open late May–mid-Sep (beach); late Nov–mid-Apr (ski resort) • Adm • www.nhstateparks.org*

4 Crawford Notch State Park
This vast wilderness is a hiker's paradise. Climb 2,804-ft (855-m) Mount Willard for great views. ⊛ *2059 Rte. 302, Hart's Location • Map M4 • 603 374 2272 • Open late May–Oct: daily • Adm • www.nhstateparks.org*

5 Children's Museum of New Hampshire
A human-sized kaleidoscope and an interactive sound sculpture are two of the imaginative exhibits. ⊛ *6 Washington St., Dover • Map N5 • 603 742 2002 • Closed Mon except in summer and school vacations • Adm • www.childrens-museum.org*

6 Wellington State Park
The huge swimming beach on Newfound Lake is a summer favorite. Hike the nature trails in the fall for the brilliant foliage. ⊛ *Rte. 3A, Bristol • Map L5 • 603 744 2197 • Open mid-May–mid-Oct: weekends only except mid-Jun–Aug daily • Adm • www.nhstateparks.org*

7 Enfield Shaker Museum
Like the furniture and tools displayed inside, the Great Stone Dwelling has an austere grace. ⊛ *447 Rte. 4A, Enfield • Map L5 • 603 632 4346 • Open daily • Adm • www.shakermuseum.org*

8 Wright Museum
This museum focuses on the heroic efforts of the US services in World War II, as well as the sacrifices on the home front. ⊛ *77 Center St., Wolfeboro • Map M5 • 603 569 1212 • Closed Nov–Jan, Feb–Apr Mon–Sat • www.wrightmuseum.org*

9 Budweiser Brewery Tour
An informative tour concludes with a tasting. The stables of the famous Clydesdale horses are a highlight. ⊛ *221 Daniel Webster Hwy., Merrimack • Map M6 • 603 595 1202 • Closed Tue & Wed Jan–Apr • Free*

10 Rhododendron State Park
Stroll along and immerse yourself in the vivid color and sweet aroma of the towering rhododendrons that bloom here in June and July. ⊛ *Rte. 119 W., Fitzwilliam • Map L6 • 603 532 8862 • Free • www.nhstateparks.org*

Left **Tubing** Center **Manchester Monarchs** Right **Cross-country skiing, White Mountains**

🔟 Winter Activities

Manchester Monarchs
A family-friendly atmosphere underscores the games of this American Hockey League affiliate of the Los Angeles Kings. ✪ *555 Elm St., Manchester • Map M6 • 603 626 7825 • Open Oct–Apr • Adm • www.manchestermonarchs.com*

Outdoor Skating
Low temperatures guarantee a long season of outdoor skating on the Schouler Park rink in this picturesque village. ✪ *Schouler Park, Main St., North Conway • Map M4 • Open Dec–Mar • Free*

Snowmobiling
Marvel at the hushed beauty of New Hampshire's snow-clad mountains in winter on a guided snowmobile tour. ✪ *Alpine Adventures, 41 Main St., Lincoln • Map L4 • 603 745 9911 • Open late Dec–Mar • Adm • www.alpinesnowmobiling.com*

SnowCoach
This special vehicle carries passengers above the treeline on Mt. Washington Auto Road for stunning winter vistas. ✪ *Great Glen Trails, Rte 16., Pinkham Notch, Gorham • Map N4 • 603 466 2333 • Open Dec–Mar daily • Adm • www.greatglentrails.com*

Snow Tubing
For old-fashioned fun, climb a snow-covered hill and then whiz back down on a cushy, oversized inner tube. ✪ *Great Glen Trails, Rte. 16, Pinkham Notch, Gorham • Map N4 • 603 466 2333 • Open Dec–Mar daily • Adm • www.greatglentrails.com*

Horse-drawn Sleigh Rides
Large sleighs depart several times daily. For romance, go for the intimate Victorian option. ✪ *Farm by the River, 2555 West Side Rd., North Conway • Map M4 • 603 356 6640 • Open Dec–Feb daily • Adm • www.farmbytheriver.com*

Dog Sledding
Alaskan huskies set off into the forested hills of Bretton Woods on trips of 20 minutes to an hour, led by experienced guides. ✪ *Mount Washington Resort, Rte. 302, Bretton Woods • Map M3 • 603 278 1000 • Open Dec–Apr daily • Adm • www.mountwashingtonresort.com*

Nordic Skiing
Glide along scenic trails at the edge of the White Mountain National Forest. The Waterville Valley Nordic Center teaches skate skiing. ✪ *Waterville Valley Resort, 1 Ski Area Rd., Waterville Valley • Map M4 • 603 236 4666 • Open Dec–Mar • Adm • www.waterville.com*

Alpine Skiing
New Hampshire's many top-class ski runs are easily reached via Rte.16 or 1-91. ✪ *Map L/M 3–4*

New England Ski Museum
The first aerial ski tramway in the US opened on Cannon Mountain in 1938. This museum traces the development of the sport. ✪ *Exit 34B I-93/Franconia Notch Parkway, Franconia • Map L3 • 603 823 7177 • Open late May–Mar daily • Free • www.skimuseum.org*

For more on skiing in New England **See pp54–5**

Left **Barley House bar** Center **Sign of the Flying Goose Brew Pub** Right **The Press Room**

TOP10 Pubs and Nightlife

1 Elm City Brewing
The four-beer sampler offers a taste of the ales, porters, and stouts brewed in this 19th-century former woolen mill. Cozy booths make it ideal for conversation. § Colony Mill Marketplace, 222 West St., Keene • Map L6

2 Harlow's Pub
Stop in at this relaxed venue on Monday nights for a bluegrass jam; or try weekends, when it might be rock and blues, reggae, or even gypsy jazz. § 3 School St., Peterborough • Map L6

3 Linda's Sports Bar
This neighborhood bar has regular pinball, pool, and darts competitions, along with four televisions tuned to sports. Check the schedule for live music, karaoke, and trivia nights. § 2b Burnham Rd., Hudson • Map M6

4 The Press Room
Still going strong after three decades, this pub features live jazz from Sunday to Tuesday. The rest of the week might bring Celtic music and sea shanties, blues, soul, folk, or even poetry. § 77 Daniel St., Portsmouth • Map N6

5 Flying Goose Brew Pub
With a schedule of live music, "the Goose" lures regulars and travelers alike for hearty traditional food, malty ales made on the premises, and lively conversation. § 40 Andover Rd., New London • Map L5

6 The Shaskeen
This atmospheric pub was founded by two Irish musicians who put equal effort into the nightly schedule of traditional Irish music and the classic Irish fare. § 909 Elm St., Manchester • Map M6

7 Patrick's Pub & Eatery
On Thursday nights, Boston comics make the trek to this lively dive, and bands keep everyone rocking on the weekends. Pints of Guinness complement the Irish-themed menu. § 18 Weirs Rd., Gilford • Map M5

8 Barley House
With a dozen fine imported and locally brewed beers on tap and a wood-paneled pub room, the Barley House feels more like a private club than a public bar. § 132 N. Main St., Concord • Map M5

9 Woodstock Inn, Station & Brewery
English malts and international hops yield a range of outstanding ales geared for hikers, skiers, and outdoors enthusiasts. § 135 Main St., N. Woodstock • Map L4

10 Moat Mountain Smoke House & Brewing Co.
This ski-country restaurant takes barbecue seriously. The brisket is Texas dry rub, the pork comes Carolina-style (vinegar doused), and ribs come St. Louis-style. Match them all with the caramel brown ale. § 3378 White Mountain Hwy., Rte. 16, N. Conway • Map M4

Price Categories

For a three course	
meal for one with half	**$** under $25
a bottle of wine (or	**$$** $25–$40
equivalent meal), taxes	**$$$** $40–$50
and extra charges.	**$$$$** $50–$65
	$$$$$ over $65

Left **Luca's Mediterranean Café** Right **Hart's Turkey Farm Restaurant**

Restaurants

Ristorante Massimo
Sophisticated, largely northern Italian dishes make great use of New England seafood, especially lobster from local waters. The romantic dining room is set in a Federal-era custom house. ⊗ *59 Penhallow St., Portsmouth • Map N6 • 603 436 4000 • Closed L, Sun • $$$$*

Black Trumpet Bistro
The chef-owner transforms local seafood and produce into lusty American bistro dishes. ⊗ *29 Ceres St., Portsmouth • Map N6 • 603 431 0887 • Closed L • $$$$*

Inn at Thorn Hill & Spa
Upscale meat-and-potatoes with a French accent head up this bold menu. Wine is taken very seriously. ⊗ *Thorn Hill Rd., Jackson • Map M3 • 603 383 4242 • Open B, L & D daily • $$$$ (D), $$$ (B, L)*

Zins Winebistro
Located at the venerable inn that serves as the center of Dartmouth College's social scene, Zins serves jazzy contemporary fare and 34 wines by the glass. ⊗ *Main St., Hanover • Map L4 • 603 643 4300 • $$$*

Luca's Mediterranean Café
Northern Italian cuisine reigns at this casual but classy trattoria, although specials may be from North Africa and the eastern Mediterranean. ⊗ *10 Central Sq., Keene • Map L6 • 603 358 3335 • Closed Apr–Dec: Sat–Sun L; Jan–Mar: Sun • $$*

Hart's Turkey Farm Restaurant
It's Thanksgiving every day at this family restaurant specializing in roast turkey dinners with all the fixings. You can also get your gobbler as a fricasee or with pasta. ⊗ *233 Daniel Webster Hwy., Rtes 3 & 104, Meredith • Map M5 • 603 279 6212 • $$*

Three Chimneys Inn
French country cooking is given a strong American accent here. ⊗ *17 Newmarket Rd., Durham • Map N6 • 603 868 7800 • Closed Sun–Mon L • $$$$*

Cotton
Start with New Hampshire's best martini, then order from the menu of updated comfort food – meatloaf and mash, steak salad, buttermilk-fried chicken – in this seriously hip spot. ⊗ *75 Arms St., Manchester • Map M6 • 603 622 5488 • Closed Sat–Sun L • $$*

Colby Hill Inn
Located in a romantic country setting, Colby Hill offers stately dining on classic New England dishes. ⊗ *3 The Oaks, Henniker • Map L5 • 603 428 3281 • Closed L; Sun brunch • $$$$*

Libby's Bistro
Creative contemporary cooking by Julia Child's former assistant has put the ski village of Gorham on the culinary map. ⊗ *111 Main St., Gorham • Map M3 • 603 466 5330 • Closed L, Mon–Tue D • $$$*

All restaurants open for lunch and dinner daily unless indicated.

Left **Belfast, Penobscot Bay** Right **Cliffs of Mount Kineo on Moosehead Lake**

Maine

Maine is New England on the grandest scale – it's larger than Connecticut, Rhode Island, Vermont, and New Hampshire combined. Much of the state remains *terra incognita* to visitors, who rarely stray far from the coastline. Of course, with a coast that wriggles around peninsulas and into harbors for an astonishing 5,500 miles (8,850 km) between Kittery and Calais, there's plenty to see without abandoning the smell of salt air. Turn off Route 1 down any peninsula, and you suddenly enter a world of broad scenic vistas and salt-sprayed small villages, with a lobster harbor at the tip. Along Maine's southern coast, shining sand beaches stretch for miles. A province of Massachusetts from 1652 to 1820, Maine was famous into the 20th century for harvesting tall timber and building tall ships. Even today, Maine's windjammer cruise fleet is one of the world's largest.

Marina and lobster boats, Kennebunk

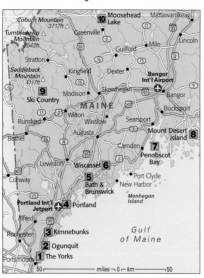

Sights

1. The Yorks
2. Ogunquit
3. Kennebunks
4. Portland and Casco Bay
5. Bath and Brunswick
6. Wiscasset
7. Penobscot Bay
8. Mount Desert Island
9. Ski Country
10. Moosehead Lake

Windjammers were the grandest of cargo sailing ships, with a large iron or steel hull, three to five large masts, and a square sail.

1 The Yorks

York has two very different faces: there's history-steeped York Village, and then there's the brassy summer playground of York Beach. Founded in 1634, York was Maine's first successful European settlement, and the Old York Historical Society's nine museum buildings chronicle more than 300 years of local history.

Ocean vista at Marginal Way, Ogunquit

Long Sands and Short Sands swimming beaches are the chief attractions at York Beach, which also boasts a carousel and arcade. Drive to the end of Cape Neddick between the beaches to see iconic Nubble Light. ◈ *Map N6 • Museums of Old York: 207 York St. and 3 Lindsay Rd.; 207 363 4974; open 9:30am–4pm Mon–Sat Jun–mid-Oct; adm; www.oldyork.org*

2 Ogunquit

Plein air painters discovered Ogunquit in the 1890s, and visitors have been seeing beauty at every turn since. Picturesque Perkins Cove, once a fishing harbor, fairly bristles with art galleries, souvenir shops, and seafood shacks. Marginal Way, a short walking path over a rocky headland just north of the cove, is lined with profusely blooming beach roses. Benches let you enjoy the ocean vistas. The path exits onto the 2-mile (3.2-km) curve of Ogunquit Beach *(see p43)*. ◈ *Map N5*

3 Kennebunks

The town of Kennebunk developed two distinct

Building in Portland's downtown arts district

villages: Kennebunk on the river, and Kennebunkport where the river meets the ocean. Once a shipbuilding center, Kennebunk has now become principally a community of summer vacation homes. Visit the Brick Store Museum for exhibits on the town's cultural and historic heritage. Then head to Dock Square in Kennebunkport to peruse the boutiques and galleries. Time permitting, stroll along the beach down Ocean Avenue toward Walker's Point, the compound of former president George H.W. Bush. ◈ *Map N5 • Brick Store Museum: 117 Main St., Kennebunk; 207 985 4802; open 10am–4:30pm Tue–Fri, 10am–1pm Sat; adm; www. brickstoremuseum.org*

4 Portland and Casco Bay

Maine's largest community has the cultural advantages of a mid-sized city and all the natural beauty of a handsome, well-protected bay. The once-bedraggled maritime district has been reborn in the animated restaurants, bars, and boutiques of the Old Port *(see pp22–3)*.

Village green, Bath

5 Bath and Brunswick

Nearly half the US ocean-going sailing vessels launched in the late 19th century went down the ways from Bath shipyards – a history detailed at the Maine Maritime Museum *(see p34)*. Nearby Brunswick is better known for making scholars than ships. Bowdoin College educated authors Nathaniel Hawthorne and Henry Wadsworth Longfellow, as well as intrepid Arctic explorers Robert Peary and Donald MacMillan. The college's Peary-MacMillan Arctic Museum *(see p49)* displays amazing photographs and artifacts from their expeditions. Map P4

6 Wiscasset

Even driving through, you'll have plenty of time to contemplate Wiscasset's self-description as "the prettiest village in Maine" because the narrow bridge across the Sheepscot River backs traffic up to a crawl in midsummer. Better

to park and walk around this stunning village where adept 18th- and 19th-century ship-wrights turned their talents to building houses for sea captains *(see p38)*. Map P4

7 Penobscot Bay

The west coast of Penobscot Bay is the best-kept secret of Maine, even though most of the state's windjammer sailing fleet *(see p56)* anchors in Rockland and Camden. Rockland is the state's lobster capital and home of the treasured Farnsworth Museum *(see p53)*; Camden has one of Maine's most beautiful harbors – a yacht-filled silver bowl at the foot of a mountain. Belfast is the hippest of the lot, a community where artists and artisans set the tone. Map Q3

8 Mount Desert Island

French explorer Samuel de Champlain pinned the name *Ile des Monts Deserts* on this large island in 1604, and "island of bare mountains" has stuck ever since. The rocky balds that Champlain observed are prized among hikers and climbers in Acadia National Park *(see pp10–11)*.

<hr>

The Maine Moose

The official state animal, the moose *(Alces alces)* is found all over Maine, with the greatest concentrations near Moosehead and Rangeley lakes. They often cross roads at dawn and dusk, so take special care driving through swampy areas. An 800-lb (363-kg) gentle giant makes a considerable impact in a collision.

Penobscot Bay

The bare peaks of Mount Desert Island were scraped clean by glaciers 10,000 years ago.

Ski Country

Moist air masses sweeping up the eastern seaboard meet the icy jet stream bringing Arctic air off the Canadian shield in northwest Maine, just east of the White Mountains. The result is massive dumps of snow which guarantee that the peaks around Bethel, Newry, Kingfield, and Jackman will be buried in the white gold that skiers crave. In the summertime, long green meadows are transformed into championship golf courses.
⊗ Map N2

Sunday River Ski Resort, near Bethel

Moosehead Lake

There's something mythic about the name of Moosehead Lake, the largest body of water contained within a single New England state. From the air, the multi-lobed lake indeed resembles the antlers of a moose, and if you take a seaplane tour, you'll almost certainly see some of these impressive creatures out for a swim (like a motorboat, they leave a wake). The lake is famed for hunting, fishing, and winter snowmobiling, but photographic moose safaris are increasingly popular. Inquire at Greenville's visitor center. ⊗ Map P1 • Visitor center: 156 Moosehead Lake Rd., Greenville; 207 695 2702; open 10am–4pm Mon–Sat year-round except Christmas and New Year; www.mooseheadlake.org

A Day's Drive in Wyeth Country

Morning

The rocky Maine coast has entranced many painters, but Andrew Wyeth (1917–2009) was among the few to chart the quiet country life of the saltwater farms. This drive shows you Maine through Wyeth's eyes. From Rte. 1 in **Waldoboro**, turn south toward the village of **Friendship**, famed for its namesake sloop. You'll see plenty of them in the harbor before continuing (north now) toward **Cushing**. The **Olson House** was made famous in Wyeth's iconic "Christina's World" (1948), and it looks little changed since Wyeth painted it. Continue north to Rte. 1, passing through handsome **Thomaston**, and turn right at High St. (Rte. 131). Enjoy stunning vistas as you drive to **Port Clyde** at the tip of the peninsula, where the Monhegan Island (see p40) ferry departs.

Afternoon

Just north of the harbor, look out for signs to **Marshall Point Lighthouse Museum**. The light was automated in 1971; volunteers staff the former keeper's house as a local history museum (see p41). Head north again toward **Tenants Harbor** for dockside lobster at **Cod End** (Commercial St.). After lunch, continue north to Rockland, to visit the **Maine Lighthouse Museum** (see p35), and spend serious time at the **Farnsworth Museum** (see p53) enjoying art by three generations of Wyeth painters along with artists who worked on Monhegan Island, and the work of modernist Louise Nevelson, who grew up in Rockland.

Left **Boothbay Harbor** Center **Old Orchard Beach** Right **Bangor**

Best of the Rest

Old Orchard Beach
This sandy beach, with its gentle surf, is the perfect place for family swimming. Kids will love the amusement park rides, the waterslide, and a pier dotted with fast food vendors and games of skill. ◈ *Map N5*

Boothbay Harbor
Regarded by many as the boating capital of midcoast Maine, this picturesque harbor is a great spot to go on a whale-watch, or to spend the day fishing. ◈ *Map P4*

Monhegan Island
Birders and hikers flock to the rocky cliffs of this offshore art colony every summer. After the tourists leave, the lobster fishermen return for the profitable winter season. ◈ *Map Q4*

Castine and Blue Hill
A drive down a single peninsula takes you to two great towns: art-minded Blue Hill, with its excellent pottery studios; and Castine, with its rich Colonial heritage and the Maine Maritime Academy. ◈ *Map Q3, R3*

Deer Isle and Stonington
Artists and fishermen seem to flock together in Maine. The Haystack Mountain School of Crafts made Deer Isle famous years ago, while the lobster boats still tend to outnumber pleasure craft in Stonington's striking harbor. ◈ *Map R3*

Lubec and Campobello Island
America's first sunrise strikes the iconic barber-pole lighthouse at West Quoddy Head in Lubec. A bridge leads to Campobello Island, where Franklin Roosevelt summered. ◈ *West Quoddy Head Light Visitor Ctr.: S. Lubec Rd. • Map R6 • 207 733 2180 • Open late May–mid-Oct daily • Free • www.westquoddy.com*

Bangor
Once the world's timber capital, handsome mansions still dot this Penobscot River town, that serves as jump-off point to the northern wilderness. ◈ *Map Q2*

Baxter State Park
Pristine forest covers 327 sq miles (848 sq km). Test your mettle by scaling 5,267-ft (1,605-m) Mount Katahdin. ◈ *64 Balsam Dr., Millinocket (office) • Map Q5 • 207 723 5140 • Closed Sat–Sun mid-Oct–late May • www.baxterstateparkauthority.com*

Rangeley Lake Region
Spruce- and hemlock-clad peaks rise with robust grace from a plateau splashed with 112 lakes and ponds, creating an outdoors enthusiast's paradise. ◈ *Map N2*

Allagash Wilderness
Forever wild, the Allagash is a legendary system of rivers and lakes where the trout (and the mosquitoes) are bigger than anywhere else. ◈ *Maine Bureau of Parks & Lands: 106 Hogan Rd., Bangor • Map Q4–5 • 207 941 4014*

Left **Schooner** Center **Boothbay Whale Watch** Right **Three Rivers Whitewater**

🔟 Boat Rides

Casco Bay Lines
On the oldest ferry service in the US, you can select sunrise, sunset, or midnight cruises. ✪ *56 Commercial St., Portland • Map N4 • 207 774 7871 • Ferry year-round; some cruises summer only • www.cascobaylines.com*

Three Rivers Whitewater
Hold on tight as your guide negotiates waves and rapids on this adrenaline-filled rafting trip down the Kennebec River. ✪ *2265 Rte. 201, The Forks • Map P1 • 207 663 2104 • Open May–Oct • Adm • Minimum age 10 • www.threeriverswhitewater.com*

S.S. Katahdin
Moosehead Lake is stunning during fall foliage. Survey the scene aboard the *S.S. Katahdin*, a 1914 steamboat. ✪ *Moosehead Marine Museum, Greenville • Map P1 • 207 695 2716 • Open late Jun–mid-Oct • Adm • www.katahdincruises.com*

Boothbay Whale Watch
A shipboard naturalist will help you identify migrating whales. You might also spot seals, porpoises, and dolphins. ✪ *Boothbay Harbor • Map P4 • 207 633 3500 • Open late May–mid-Oct • Adm • www.whaleme.com*

Monhegan Boat Line
Drift past lobster boats on the trip from Port Clyde to Monhegan Island. Or opt for a cruise past the Muscongus Bay lighthouses. ✪ *Port Clyde • Map Q4 • 207 372 8848 • Closed Sun in winter • Adm • www.monheganboat.com*

Schooner Appledore
Get your sea legs with day sails around Penobscot Bay on this 86-footer. ✪ *Bayview Landing, Camden • Map Q3 • 207 236 8353 • Open Jun–Oct • Adm • www.appledore2.com*

Maine Adventure Sails
Sail aboard National Historic Landmark pilot schooner *Timberwind* for three- to six-day trips around midcoast Maine. ✪ *Rockport • Map Q3 • 800 759 9250 • Open late May–early Oct • www.maineadventuresails.com*

Downeast Windjammer Cruises
The 151-ft (46-m) *Margaret Todd* makes three trips a day through the islands of Frenchman Bay. ✪ *Bar Harbor Inn Pier, Bar Harbor • Map R3 • 207 288 4585 • Open May–Oct • Adm • www.downeastwindjammer.com*

Bold Coast Charter Company
About 3,000 endangered puffins gather on Machias Seal Island. Bold Coast offers the only sightseeing trips for birdwatchers and photographers. ✪ *JCutler Harbor • Map R6 • Open Jun–mid-Aug • Adm • Reservations essential • www.boldcoast.com*

Allagash Canoe Trips
The Allagash River and Chamberlain Lake offer paddling journeys in pristine North Woods wilderness. There's also good trout fishing. ✪ *Map Q5 • 207 280 1551 • Open Jul–Aug, Oct • Adm • Apply on website • www.allagashcanoetrips.com*

Around New England – Maine

Left **Trenton Bridge Lobster Pound** Center **Barnacle Billy's** Right **The Clam Shack**

📖10 Lobster Pounds

1 Five Islands Lobster Co.
Lobstermen stream in all day as diners at picnic tables crack lobsters, dip the meat in melted butter, and enjoy the view of a perfect harbor. ⊗ *1447 Five Islands Rd., Georgetown • Map P4 • 207 371 2990 Closed mid-Oct–early May • $$*

2 The Clam Shack
The namesake fried clams are always good, but the real specialty here is the lobster roll. ⊗ *On the Bridge, Kennebunkport • Map N5 • 207 967 3321 • Closed mid-Oct– mid-May • $*

3 The Lobster Pound
Take a quick dip, then sit on the deck of this classic seafood restaurant to break down a boiled lobster dinner – or dine inside to escape mendicant gulls. ⊗ *Rte. 1, Lincolnville Beach • Map Q3 • 207 789 5550 • Closed mid-Oct–mid-May • $*

4 Barnacle Billy's
The bargain-hunter's choice in a pricey resort, Billy's has both a full-service restaurant and a bare-bones seafood shack, on scenic Perkins Cove. ⊗ *Perkins Cove Rd., Ogunquit • Map N5 • 207 646 5575 • Closed Nov–mid-Apr • $*

5 Shaw's Fish & Lobster Wharf
A lobster fan's nirvana, Shaw's has spectacular views of the working harbor, a raw bar, and a full liquor license. ⊗ *Rte. 32, New Harbor • Map P4 • 207 677 2200 • Closed mid-Oct–mid-May • $$*

6 Boothbay Lobster Wharf
On one of Maine's legendary lobstering harbors, the Lobster Wharf has the shortest possible distance from trap to plate. Eat indoors only if it rains. ⊗ *97 Atlantic Ave., Boothbay Harbor • Map P4 • 207 633 4900 • Closed mid-Oct–mid-May • $$*

7 Trenton Bridge Lobster Pound
Lobster, nutcrackers, picks, and heaps of paper napkins are really all you need, and this pound barely on the mainland side from Mount Desert Island is a bargain spot for authentic experiences. BYOB. ⊗ *1237 Bar Harbor Rd., Trenton • Map R3 • 207 667 2977 • Closed mid- Oct–late Apr • $$*

8 Bayley's Lobster Pound
Founded in 1915, there are some great specialties here, like lobster-stuffed mushrooms and excellent crabcakes. ⊗ *9 Avenue 6, Pine Point, Scarborough • Map N5 • 207 883 4571 • Closed mid-Oct–late Apr • $*

9 Cape Neddick Harborside Restaurant
Sample the steamed mussels or clams here first, before cracking into the main attraction. ⊗ *60 Shore Rd., Cape Neddick • Map N5 • 207 363 5471 • Ring for winter hours • $$$*

10 Cook's Lobster House
Enjoy your lobster surround- ed on three sides by water, with a view of the world's only crib- stone bridge. ⊗ *Rte. 24, Bailey Island • Map P4 • 207 833 2818 • $$*

All pounds serve lunch and dinner. Many open weekends from mid- Apr; close Mon–Wed after Labor Day; then close for season mid-Oct.

Price Categories

For a three course meal for one with half a bottle of wine (or equivalent meal), taxes and extra charges.

$	under $25
$$	$25–$40
$$$	$40–$50
$$$$	$50–$65
$$$$$	over $65

Left **Cinque Terre** Right **Arrows Restaurant**

⁑10 Restaurants

Dockside
An island location in York Harbor makes fish the natural dish, from haddock, cod, and lobster to diver scallops and clams from nearby beds. Bouillabaisse of Maine seafood is always a good bet. 🕲 *Harris Island Rd., York • Map N5 • 207 363 2868 • Closed Nov–May • $$$*

Moody's Diner
Vacationers and Mainers rub elbows in this iconic diner. Try the blueberry muffins, or the turkey dinner followed by walnut pie. 🕲 *Rte. 1, Waldoboro • Map Q3 • 207 832 7785 • Open B, L, D daily • $$*

Primo Restaurant
The chef here conjures up culinary wonders from mostly home-grown produce – even Brussels sprouts get to be stars in season. 🕲 *2 S. Main St., Rockland • Map Q3 • 207 596 0770 • Closed L, Tue, ring for winter hours • $$$$$*

White Barn Inn
Two 1820s barns make a surprisingly elegant and restful space in which to enjoy the four-course tasting menu. 🕲 *37 Beach Ave., Kennebunkport • Map N5 • 207 967 2321 • Closed L • $$$$$ • Reservations essential; jacket required for men*

Cinque Terre
Much of the organic produce that goes into the spectacular Ligurian-coast dishes is grown on site. 🕲 *36 Wharf St., Portland • Map N4 • 207 347 6154 • Closed L, Mon–Tue D; winter hours vary • $$$*

Chase's Daily
Back-to-the-land farmers launched this high quality bakery-restaurant-art gallery. 🕲 *96 Main St., Belfast • Map Q3 • 207 338 0555 • Open Tue–Sat L, Fri D, Sun brunch • $$*

Fore Street
Sample the wildly popular wood-oven roasted mussels from a menu built largely around local ingredients. 🕲 *288 Fore St., Portland • Map N4 • 207 775 2717 • Closed L • $$$$ • Reservations essential*

Robinhood Free Meetinghouse
An 1855 meeting house makes a graceful setting for contemporary French dining. Patrons crave the chef's 72-layer cream cheese biscuits. 🕲 *210 Robinhood Rd., Georgetown • Map P4 • 207 371 2188 • Closed L, winter hours vary • $$$$ • Reservations essential*

Rupununi
This American bar and grill has lobster for seafood fans, steaks and burgers for landlubbers. 🕲 *119 Maine St., Bar Harbor • Map R3 • 207 288 2886 • Closed Nov–Apr • $$$*

Arrows Restaurant
The fairytale setting of an 18th-century farmhouse and bounteous summer gardens bring the spirit and style of Napa to the Maine countryside. 🕲 *Berwick Rd., Ogunquit • Map N5 • 207 361 1100 • Closed L & Jan–mid-Apr; call for schedule • $$$$$*

Many native Mainers eat early; dinner often begins at 5pm. All restaurants open for lunch and dinner daily unless indicated.

Left **Edgecomb Potters Gallery & Studio Complex** Right **Bluejacket Ship Crafters**

Artisan Shops

1. Maine Balsam Fir Products

This rustic shop in the Oxford Hills specializes in handmade balsam-filled pillows, and balsam oil and soap, all with the bracing scent of Maine's woods. ✆ *16 Morse Hill Rd., West Paris • Map N3*

2. Thomas Moser Cabinetmakers

You might pick up some home decorating tips in this restored 19th-century home, where contemporary paintings and photography are displayed next to the cabinetmakers' furniture. ✆ *149 Main St., Freeport • Map P4*

3. Edgecomb Potters Gallery & Studio Complex

Richly colored glazes are the hallmark of Edgecomb porcelain, which is on sale with work by other artisans, working in wood, metal, and glass. ✆ *727 Boothbay Rd., Rte. 27S, Edgecomb • Map P4*

4. Swans Island Blankets

A Swans Island blanket is the ultimate cold-weather luxury. The showroom-studio is set in a converted 1780s farmhouse. ✆ *321 Rte. 1, Northport • Map Q3*

5. Bluejacket Ship Crafters

The oldest ship-modeling company in the US has more than 100 historically accurate examples on display. Select a kit for a sailing sloop, or radio-controlled lobster boat. ✆ *160 E. Main St., Searsport • Map Q3*

6. Weathervanes of Maine

Weathervanes once topped every Maine barn. This company helps keep the tradition alive, with its menagerie of hand-crafted copper animals, from a jaunty rooster to a flying pig. ✆ *1451 Rte. 1, Wells • Map Q3*

7. Eggemoggin Textile Studio

Chris Leith's woven scarves, shawls, and capes draw their inspiration from the ever-changing ocean at Eggemoggin Reach, and the earthy reds and browns of the shore's blueberry barrens. ✆ *497 Reach Rd., Sedgwick • Map R3*

8. Rackliffe Pottery

Stop off at this workshop overlooking Blue Hill Bay and you might see artisans throwing dishware on a potter's wheel. A blueberry bowl makes a perfect souvenir of Maine. ✆ *Ellsworth Rd., Blue Hill • Map R3*

9. Abbe Museum

The gift shop of this small museum has highly prized sweetgrass, ash, and birchbark baskets, made by Maine's Native peoples. ✆ *26 Mount Desert St., Rte. 3, Bar Harbor • Map R3*

10. Columbia Falls Pottery

It seems as if the artists simply look out the window for inspiration for their tiles, clocks, lamps, and crocks, all decorated with painted blueberries, lupines, sailboats, and shore birds. ✆ *150 Main St., Columbia Falls • Map R6*

Many shops keep shorter hours in winter; check ahead.

Left **Blacksmith's Mall** Center **Marston House Antiques** Right **Antiques USA**

🔟 Antiques Shops

York Antiques Gallery
Dealers here specialize in fine 18th- and 19th-century furniture and accessories. You probably won't find a bargain, but you might pick up decorating ideas. ⬥ *746 Rte. 1, York • Map N5*

Blacksmith's Mall
After a morning on Ogunquit beach, peruse the offerings in this nearby shop. Dealers lean toward small objects of desire – jewelry, glass, porcelain, linens, and nifty kitchen items. ⬥ *166 Main St., Ogunquit • Map N5*

Douglas N. Harding Rare Books
You'll find volumes on everything from circus arts to UFOs in this 14-room shop with more than 100,000 used and rare books. ⬥ *2152 Post Rd., Rte. 1, Wells • Map N5*

Wells-Union Antiques
Each of the nine shops in this inviting complex has a distinctive personality, with offerings from formal furnishings to shabby-chic accessories, and architectural ornaments to garden statuary. ⬥ *1755 Post Rd., Rte. 1, Wells • Map N5*

Victorian Lighting
Despite the name, this illuminating shop carries high-quality lighting fixtures from the 1840s right through to the 1930s, restored and rewired for modern homes. Select a simple sconce or a showpiece chandelier. ⬥ *29 York St., Rte. 1, Kennebunk • Map N5*

Antiques USA
Route 1 from York to Arundel is dense with antiques shops. Antiques USA is one of the largest, bringing hundreds of dealers with different tastes and interests under one roof. ⬥ *Rte. 1, Arundel • Map N5*

Marston House Antiques
The proprietors also own a home in a French village, so the shop's soft linens, clay pots, wire garden stands, and stoneware serving pieces all have Gallic flair. ⬥ *Main St., Wiscasset • Map P4*

Pumpkin Patch Antiques
Country furniture and a lovely selection of mid-20th-century quilts highlight the domestic antiques in this small shop. Nautical items and Chinese porcelain are reminders of Searsport's maritime heyday. ⬥ *15 Rte. 1, Searsport • Map Q3*

Leila Day Antiques
Soak up the history of this 1797 home, as you view the furniture, Chinese porcelain, nautical items, folk art, and 19th- and 20th-century paintings. ⬥ *53 Main St., Castine • Map Q3*

Big Chicken Barn
The proprietors of this gigantic emporium encourage browsers to bring a picnic lunch. It takes hours to peruse the thousands of magazines, rare books, and antiques. ⬥ *1768 Bucksport Rd., Ellsworth • Map R3*

STREETSMART

NEW ENGLAND'S TOP 10

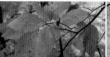

Left **US money** Center **Fall foliage is a big visitor draw** Right **US electrical plug for cellphone**

Planning Your Trip

1 Passports/Visas

Everyone entering the US must have a machine-readable biometric passport. Citizens of the EU and other visa-waiver countries must apply for entry at least 72 hours ahead of travel.
🌐 https://esta.cbp.dhs.gov

2 Tourism Information

Discover New England focuses the tourism resources of the six New England states. 🌐 www. discovernewengland.org

3 When to Go

New England is a year-round destination, but traffic is heaviest from late June through mid-October; and from Christmas through late February in ski country. Bargains can often be had from late April into late May, and in late October, but some rural attractions will only open weekends.

4 Weather

New England weather varies widely. Daytime temperatures from December to February are usually freezing or colder, while July and August daytime highs often exceed 80°F (26.7°C), with high humidity. September and October are usually cool and dry, while November and March are chilly and damp. Spring weather ranges from warm sun to windy rain. Northerly areas are generally 10°F (7°C) cooler.

5 What to Pack

Given the changeable weather, it makes sense to dress in layers, with a sweater or jacket for cool summer evenings. Be sure to pack a folding umbrella, sunglasses, and comfortable walking shoes. You may want to pack smart-casual outfits for restaurants and evening entertainment. In midwinter, a warm coat, scarf, gloves, and a hat that protects your ears are necessities, and boots are recommended.

6 Time Zone

New England is in the Eastern time zone: GMT minus five hours. Daylight saving time (EDT) begins at 2am on the second Sunday in March and reverts to standard time (EST) at 2am on the first Sunday in November. During EDT, the local time is GMT minus four hours.

7 Currency

US money comes in dollars and cents. Coins come in 1-, 5-, 10-, 25-, and 50-cent, and 1-dollar denominations. Dollar coins are used mostly in vending machines; 50-cent pieces are rare. The quarter (25-cent piece) is the handiest coin for vending machines and parking meters. Notes (bills) are $1, $5, $10, $20, $50, and $100, though a few $2 bills are still in circulation. Small businesses often decline $50 and $100 bills.

8 Insurance

It's a good idea to buy comprehensive travel insurance prior to your departure. Emergency medical or dental treatment is expensive, and proof of insurance is all but mandatory. A good policy will also pay to replace lost or stolen property. If you need to cancel or change your travel plans, many policies will refund your costs.

9 Current and Phone Adapters

US electricity is 110–120 volts, 60 cycles, and uses a polarized two-prong plug. To use non-US appliances you will need an adapter and voltage converter, available at airport shops and some department and electrical stores. Most laptops and travel appliances are dual-voltage, and many hotels have dual-voltage sockets for electric shavers. US phone systems use an RJ11 connector.

10 Special Equipment

If you're planning to do a lot of hiking, or walking in the woods, lightweight collapsible trekking poles are a good investment. Sold in pairs for mountain trekking, a set will equip two people with walking sticks. Good binoculars greatly enhance the pleasure of watching wildlife, and may be less expensive to purchase in the US.

Travelers visiting the USA under the visa waiver program must complete an online ESTA form before departure.

Left **Smoking regulations** Center **Weights and measures** Right **Tipping**

Useful Information

Useful Websites
Yankee Magazine's online guide (www.newengland.com), the *Boston Globe*'s website (www.bostonglobe.com), and the Boston CVB site (www.bostonusa.com) are all valuable sources of information.

Opening Hours
Most stores and attractions open daily, although many museums close Mondays. Some banks open on Saturday morning, but most close weekends. Hours and days of opening may be abbreviated in winter – check with venues.

Public Holidays
As well as Christmas and New Year, these major holidays are marked throughout New England: Martin Luther King Day (3rd Mon in Jan); Presidents' Day (3rd Mon in Feb); Memorial Day (last Mon in May); Independence Day (4 Jul); Labor Day (1st Mon in Sep); Columbus Day (2nd Mon in Oct); Veterans' Day (11 Nov); Thanksgiving (4th Thu in Nov). Banks and government offices are closed, alcohol sales may be curtailed, and many shops also close.

Smoking
Smoking is generally prohibited in most indoor locations, and in some outdoor ones, such as sports arenas and playgrounds; always check for "no smoking" signs before lighting up. Tobacco products cannot be sold to under-18s.

Consulates
Most consulates in New England are based in Boston. They cannot intervene in legal matters, but they can provide limited services and referrals for visiting nationals.

Tipping
Plan to tip for most services: 15–20 per cent for waitstaff; $1 per bag for porters; $2 to valet parking attendants; 50 cents to $1 per drink to bartenders; and 10 per cent of the fare (rounded up to the next dollar) for taxi drivers.

Sales Periods
Household linens are often discounted at January "white sales," winter apparel in March to April, and summer apparel in September.

Tax Rates
Stated prices rarely include taxes. All New England states except New Hampshire charge a sales tax on goods (6–7 percent), and all states charge taxes on meals (5–9 per cent) and lodgings (8–13 per cent). Many accommodations tack on surcharges for housekeeping, parking, or recreational facilities that can add up quickly. Inquire about such fees when you book.

Weights and Measures
The US follows the so-called "English system" of weights and measures. Weights are expressed in ounces, 16 of which make a pound (454 g). Volume is measured by the fluid ounce (29.6 ml). The US pint is 16 fl oz, or 473 ml. The US quart is 946 ml. The US gallon equals approximately 3.8 liters.

Public Restrooms
Airports, train stations, bus stations, and public libraries generally have free public restrooms, as do designated rest stops on major highways.

Consulates

Canada
3 Copley Pl., Suite 400, Boston, MA 02116
• 617 262 3760

United Kingdom
600 Atlantic Ave., Boston, MA 02210
• 617 245 4500

Ireland
535 Boylston St., Boston, MA 02116
• 617 267 9330

Australia
150 E. 42d St., 34th Fl., New York NY 10017
• 212 351 6500

New Zealand
222 E. 41st St., Suite 2510, New York, NY 10017 • 212 832 4038

Streetsmart

Left **Train station, North Conway** Right **Logan Airport bus**

TOP 10 Getting to New England

1 By Air
Boston's Logan International Airport (BOS) is the principal gateway airport to New England. Boston's large college population pushes flights to capacity around school holidays, and in May and September; fall foliage season is also tight.

2 Security
Security is a high priority at New England airports. Pack carry-on liquids in 3 oz or 100 ml containers in clear plastic quart or liter bags. Make sure all baggage, including carry-on, is clearly marked with ID. Keep a calm demeanor, and do not even joke about terrorism or plane crashes.

3 Logan International
Logan, just 3 miles (4.8 km) from downtown Boston, is a pleasant and efficient airport with ample parking. International flights arrive at Terminal E but may depart from other terminals. The quickest and cheapest trip into the city is via Silver Line buses to South Station; there are ticket kiosks near most terminal exits. ✆ 800 235 6426 • www.massport.com

4 Other New England Airports
A few international flights land at Connecticut's Bradley International (BDL). The Providence, Rhode Island, area and Manchester, New Hampshire, airports (PVD; MHT) often have the cheapest domestic air fares to New England. Portland Jetport (PWM) is a good Maine gateway for domestic airlines. ✆ Bradley International Airport, Windsor Locks, CT: 860 292 2000; www.bradleyairport.com • Manchester Boston Regional Airport, Manchester, NH; 603 624 6556; www.flymanchester. com • T.F. Green Airport, Warwick, RI: 401 737 8222; www.pvdairport.com • Portland Jetport, Portland, ME: 207 774 7301; www.portlandjetport.org

5 Online Air Deals
Cheapflights.com checks more airlines than other consolidators and will give you an overview of what's available, but the best rates are usually on the carriers' own websites; check both.

6 By Ship
More than a dozen cruise lines call at the Boston Cruiseport. ✆ Cruiseport Boston, 1 Black Falcon Ave., Boston, MA • Map F3 • 617 330 1500 • www.massport.com

7 By Train
Amtrak serves coastal and central New England as far north as Portland, Maine. Travelers from overseas can buy rail passes for discounted Amtrak travel throughout the US. ✆ 800 872 7245 • www.amtrak.com

8 By Bus
Concord Coach Lines serves New Hampshire and Maine; Plymouth & Brockton covers southeastern Massachusetts; Peter Pan has stops in western Massachusetts and Connecticut; National carrier Greyhound and its subsidiaries go almost everywhere. ✆ Concord: 800 639 3317; www.concordcoachlines.com • Plymouth & Brockton: 508 746 0378; www.p-b.com • Peter Pan: 800 343 9999; www.peterpanbus.com • Greyhound: 800 231 2222; www.greyhound.com

9 By Car
From the south, I-95 follows the coast to Boston, then heads north through New Hampshire to Maine. From the west, I-90 enters Massachusetts from New York State and ends at Logan Airport. From the northwest, I-89 and I-91 enter Vermont from Quebec. I-89 cuts southeast to Boston; I-91 goes south to New York via Massachusetts and Connecticut.

10 Customs
Visitors over 21 may bring two pints (1 l) of alcohol; 200 cigarettes, 50 cigars, or 4 lb (2 kg) of smoking tobacco; and gifts worth up to $100. Meats, fresh cheeses, live plants, and produce are prohibited. Travelers bringing $10,000 or more in cash must declare the money at customs.

Installation of high-speed trains has cut the service between New York's Penn Station and Boston's South Station to 4 hours or less.

Left **Boston subway** Right **Inter-island ferry from Portland**

Getting Around New England

By Train
Amtrak runs a fast service between New York and Boston, with connections running to Portland, Providence, Springfield, Hartford, St. Albans, and Burlington.

By Bus
Most cities have a local bus service. Inter-city bus transport can be arranged on the lines indicated opposite.

By Ferry
Ferries are essential for visiting islands *(see pp40–41)*, but Boston is also served by commuter ferries from the North and South Shores. They are operated by Boston Harbor Cruises for the Metropolitan Boston Transit Authority, or by the MBTA *(see below)*. ✆ *MBTA • www.mbta.com*

By Car
In Boston, driving is best left to taxi drivers. In the rest of New England, however, it is usually the best way to get around, see the countryside, stop when you want to, and explore the bywas and rural backroads *(see p132)*.

By Metro
Boston is the only New England city with a subway and light rail system. The "T" (as it is called locally) has a stop within a few blocks of almost every central city attraction, and extends into the suburbs, often as above-ground light rail. Rechargeable Charlie Cards are available at many subway stations. Charlie Card holders pay about 15 per cent less for each ride, and the card also works for buses and harbor ferries. Visitors can also purchase a LinkPass for either one or seven days' travel on metro, bus, inner harbor ferry, and the inner ring of commuter rail. ✆ *MBTA • 617 222 5000 • www. mbta.com*

Regional Airlines
New England is too small to sustain many regional carriers, but Cape Air flies small planes frequently between Boston, Nantucket, and Martha's Vineyard. In summer, there are flights to Boston from Vermont, New Hampshire, and Maine. ✆ *508 771 6944 • www.flycapeair.com*

Bicycling
Cycling is a marvelous way to explore the New England countryside. Dedicated trails of former railroad rights-of-way are found throughout the region. The national Rails to Trails Conservancy maintains a useful web-site. When sharing the roads, try to stay on the right-hand shoulder to avoid being hit. All New England states mandate the use of helmets for children under 12. ✆ *www.traillink.com*

Walking
Many towns maintain scenic walking paths; some link communities together along trails that can stretch as far as 30 miles (48 km). To explore what might be available in the area you're visiting, go to the web-site of American Trails for regional links within the state trails section. ✆ *www.americantrails.org*

Hiking
Hiking can be a satisfying way to traverse New England, providing that you are both fit and properly equipped. The main long-distance trail through the region is the Appalachian Trail, which largely sticks to the backwoods and follows some of the highest ridges in New England. If you're going to tackle it, consider joining the Appalachian Mountain Club, and purchasing relevant maps and trail guides. ✆ *800 372 1758 • www.outdoors.org*

Maps
Good highway maps are available free at state welcome centers on interstate highways – usually shortly after entering the state. For exploring in greater depth, Maine-based DeLorme publishes an excellent series of large-format atlases and gazetteers for each state. ✆ *800 561 5105 • www. delorme.com*

Established in 1897 to supplant horse-drawn streetcars, the "T" is North America's oldest subway system.

Left **Self-service gas pump** Center **Speed limit sign** Right **Moose crossing sign**

TOP 10 Driving Tips

1 Driver's License
To operate a motor vehicle in any of the New England states you will need a current driver's license from your home state or country. Most rental agencies also ask to see the passports of foreign nationals.

2 Renting a Car
Most cities have car rental agencies, but the fullest choice is at airports. Drivers must be between the ages of 25 and 75. Apart from your driver's license, you will need a major credit card as a deposit (very few rental agencies accept cash). Even if you are covered under your personal insurance, you should generally accept the Collision (or Loss) Damage Waiver to avoid financial entanglements in case of an accident.

3 Fuel
Most motor vehicles in New England run on 87 octane "regular" gasoline (petrol). Fuel is sold by the gallon and is usually pumped by the driver after leaving cash or a credit card with an attendant. If driving in winter, be sure to have a full tank before setting out in case of emergency.

4 Speed Limits
Speed limits (always in miles per hour) vary widely. Limited-access highway speeds are generally 55–65 mph;

other highways 40–55 mph. Municipal speed limits are 20–30 mph.

5 Parking
Parking is extremely limited in urban areas; many zones are reserved for residents with permits. Meter parking is usually 25 cents to a dollar per hour. Most meters only accept quarters; some will also take credit cards.

6 Traffic Circles
By law, vehicles already on the circle always have the right of way. However, in practice, never assume the other driver will do the right thing.

7 Traffic Signals
Traffic signals are uniform throughout New England: stop on red, go on green, use caution on amber. A dual amber and red light indicates a pedestrian crossing. All New England states permit a right turn on red after coming to a complete stop and ensuring that there is no oncoming traffic.

8 School Zones and Pedestrians
Not all states give pedestrians the automatic right of way, but it's best to let walkers safely cross, even if they are not in marked crosswalks. Always stop at least 100 ft (30 m) from a stopped school bus, especially if its flashers are operating.

9 Weather
Snow and ice make driving treacherous. Slow down and keep a greater-than-usual distance from the vehicle ahead of you. Be aware that road surfaces on bridges may be glare ice when the surrounding highway is otherwise fine. If you're renting a vehicle, make sure you have a spare tire, jack, and road flares in case of breakdown.

10 Wildlife
There are many wild animals in New England's countryside. Brake but do not swerve for small animals like chipmunks and squirrels. Anything larger (like a deer) could cause serious damage on impact; slow down and be prepared to stop.

Car Rentals

Avis
800 331 1212
• www.avis.com

Budget
800 527 7000
• www.budget.com

Enterprise
800 736 8222
• www.enterprise.com

Hertz
800 654 3131
• www.hertz.com

National
800 227 7368
• www.nationalcar.com

Thrifty
800 847 4389
• www.thrifty.com

American Automobile Association (AAA) services are reciprocal with British AA.

Left **ATM** Center **Wi-Fi hotspot sign** Right **Rural post office**

🔟 Banking and Communications

Banking Hours
Most banks open 9am to 2pm or later (many to 5pm) Monday to Friday; 9am to noon Saturday.

Currency Exchange
Currency exchange is available at main branches of large Boston banks, but harder to find elsewhere. In general, you will get a better rate making ATM withdrawals than exchanging cash, even with the additional banking fees.

Travelers' Checks
Dollar-denominated travelers' checks issued by American Express or Thomas Cook are widely accepted. Personal checks drawn on foreign banks – or even out-of-state banks – are not.

ATMs
ATMs are usually found near the entrances to bank offices. The main bank systems honored are Cirrus, Plus, and NYCE. Most ATMs also accept MasterCard and Visa credit cards. Many shops let you pay with a debit card and get cash back – usually a fee-free way to get ready money.

Credit Cards
Using credit cards is safer than carrying cash, and essential for renting a car or reserving a hotel room. MasterCard and Visa are almost universally accepted, as is the Discover card. Diners Club is accepted at some higher-end establishments. American Express is widely accepted, but small merchants balk at the company's high fees.

Post Offices
Most post offices are open 8am to 6pm Monday to Friday; 8am to noon Saturday. Properly stamped letters and packages less than 12 oz (340 g) can be dropped into blue mailboxes. For current rates, see the US Postal Service web site.
🌐 www.usps.com

Internet Access
Many hotels, B&Bs, and even motels offer Internet access for travelers carrying their own computers. High-speed access generally requires an Ethernet card (for corded connections) or a Wi-Fi card. Free wireless networks are often found at coffee shops and bookstores.

Telephones
Public telephones are fading fast as cellphones become ubiquitous. When you can find a pay phone, it usually accepts coins, charging 50 cents to $1 for a local call. The least expensive way to call is by using a prepaid calling card available at gas stations, convenience stores, and newsstands. Note that Boston-area calls require dialing the area code in addition to the 7-digit phone number. Dial 1 for long-distance in the US and Canada, or 011 for calls to other countries. Note that many Target, WalMart, and Radio Shack stores sell disposable cellphones for as little as $15; calling minutes cost extra.

Newspapers
Though the dominant newspaper in the region is the *Boston Globe*, the *New York Times*, *Wall Street Journal*, and *USA Today* are also widely read. For entertainment listings outside Boston, check local papers.

Television
All US broadcasters now use digital television signals. Most lodgings with TV provide "basic" cable that includes local stations, broadcast networks, and a handful of cable-only channels.

Financial Services

American Express Helpline
800 221 7282

American Express Travel Service
800 327 2177

Cirrus/MasterCard
800 424 7787

Plus/Visa
800 847 2911

Thomas Cook MasterCard Customer Services
800 223 7373

Travelex
800 287 7362

 Banks near the Canadian border without currency exchange offices will nonetheless usually exchange Canadian currency.

Left **Sunbathing on Hammonasset Beach** Center **Swimming prohibition** Right **Police car**

🔟 Security and Health

1 Security Tips
Make sure you know the escape route from your hotel room in case of fire. Secure your door with a chain and use the peephole to confirm the identity of anyone who knocks. Keep valuables in the room- or hotel-safe. Keep a separate copy of your credit card numbers and the helpline numbers in case of loss or theft.

2 Crime
Contrary to what foreigners may surmise from US television dramas, the incidence of thefts, muggings, murder, and other mayhem is low in the US in general, and even lower in New England. Nonetheless, don't court trouble. Avoid poorly lit and deserted areas such as Boston Common late at night. Know where you are going, and walk purpose-fully. Keep only small amounts of cash in your pockets. If confronted by a mugger, give up your money promptly.

3 Police
If you are stopped by the police, you are entitled to see official identification. Answer any questions truthfully, calmly, and cooperatively. American police are generally armed with guns or electric shock weapons, but most officers go through their careers without ever using them.

4 Emergency Phone Number
For police, fire, or ambulance, dial 911. Stay on the line even if you are unable to speak so that the emergency locator system can track you. Emergency calls are free.

5 Crossing Roads
In theory, pedestrians on a marked crosswalk always have the right of way, but don't count on drivers, especially those making turns, to stop for you. Also beware of bicyclists, since many do not follow the traffic rules. Be careful crossing roads at night or in bad weather, especially if your clothes do not make you visible to oncoming traffic. Your mother was right: look both ways before crossing.

6 Insect-borne Diseases
Three insect-borne infectious diseases have been reported in New England: Lyme disease, eastern equine encephalitis, and West Nile virus. Chances for exposure are slim. Lyme disease is usually spread by tick bites; the others by mosquitoes. Use insect repellent, and keep arms, legs, and ankles covered.

7 Sun Care
New England's relatively high latitude is no protection against sunburn at any time of the year. Avoid prolonged exposure, especially during the summer, and wear sunscreen of at least SPF 15.

8 Hypothermia
Chilling of the body below normal range, or hypothermia, is more common in New England in summer than winter. Most people dress warmly for cold weather, but many do not realize how quickly they can lose body heat to cold water. Swimming in cold ocean water can be refreshing on a hot day, but you should leave the water if you become chilled. A common first sign of hypothermia is blue lips; if you have them, get to a warm place, bundle up, and drink hot liquids.

9 Prescriptions
It's always a good idea to bring extra medications with you, but you should also carry a copy of your prescriptions. Ask your hotel to refer you to the nearest pharmacy.

10 Water Quality (Swimming)
Ocean and lake waters are generally clean throughout New England, though ocean beaches are sometimes closed due to runoff after storms or to the annual algae bloom known as "red tide," which produces a toxin. Beach waters are tested regularly; any closures will be prominently posted.

Left **Poison Ivy** Right **Contaminated shellfish**

TOP 10 Things to Avoid

1 Contaminated Shellfish

Food poisoning from contaminated shellfish is rare but not unheard of in New England. The authorities monitor water quality where clams, mussels, and oysters grow, and will ban them from sale during outbreaks of "red tide." If ordering steamed shellfish, do not eat any that do not open when steamed. Lobster must be cooked alive. A cooked lobster without a curled tail is not safe to eat.

2 Rush-hour Traffic

The morning and evening commutes (8–9:30am; 4–6:30pm) can add an hour to your travel time around metropolitan areas. Try to avoid traveling during those times.

3 Standing in Line

If you make restaurant reservations in advance, you can avoid up to an hour's waiting time at popular eateries. If catching a show, concert, or movie, purchase your tickets in person earlier in the day and bypass the "will-call" line or the ticket queue.

4 Ticket Scalpers

The states differ on the legality of ticket resales, but you can generally assume that anyone hawking tickets outside a popular sports or concert venue is expecting to turn a tidy profit at your expense.

Often, these tickets are bogus reproductions – but by the time you are refused entry, the seller will be long gone.

5 Dangerous Animals

Never touch a wild animal. Any wild animal in New England that accepts the approach of a human being is ill, and therefore potentially dangerous. Health authorities assume that all wild animal bites are from a rabid animal, and treat accordingly. The New England woods contain many predators (wolves, coyotes, bears, bobcats, Canadian lynx, and so on), but you are safe if you give them a wide berth. If camping, store your food securely.

6 Bottled Water

Tap water is safe to drink throughout New England. If you wish to carry bottled water with you while hiking, buy a single bottle when you arrive, then refill it regularly from the tap.

7 Recreational Drugs

Although state laws regarding cannabis use are not as strict as they once were, the purchase, sale, or use of illegal drugs can land you in jail – often for a long time. Penalties are especially harsh if transactions take place anywhere near a school or playground.

8 Poisonous Plants

Many seemingly edible plants are not. Be especially careful with berries and mushrooms, some of which can be highly toxic. Poison ivy, which causes an extremely irritating skin rash in most people but can be life-threatening to a few, is very common in New England. It has leaves in clusters of three, but can be a vine, a shrub, or low-lying growth. Stay on marked trails and remember this rule of thumb: "Leaves of three, let it be." Avoid all nettles, as stinging nettle is also common.

9 Non-Central "In-town" Hotels

Online booking engines often list hotels as being "downtown" when they are, in fact, many miles away. If in doubt, use an online mapping program to check walking directions from the hotel to a known landmark.

10 Pickpockets and Bag-snatchers

Pay attention to your surroundings. Thieves usually target people who are distracted – checking a map, talking on their cell phones, or watching a street performer. Do not set down backpacks, camera bags, or purses unless they are attached to you by a strap. Lifting a bag off a chair is child's play for a professional thief.

Left **Boston gay community newspaper** Center **Disabled parking sign** Right **Recreational cycling**

Special Concerns and Interests

1 Students
If you are a non-US student you should buy an International Student Identification Card before traveling to New England, for numerous discounts at hostels, museums, and theaters. US students can use their student ID cards for the same discounts. Young travelers should carry their passports or driver's license for entry to bars and to purchase alcohol at restaurants.
◈ www.istc.org

2 Seniors
Seniors are eligible for discounts on car rentals, National Park entrance fees, and many museums. Contact the American Association for Retired Persons (AARP) for more information. Boston-based Road Scholar offers educational programs with discounted lodging as well as field trips for travelers over age 55. ◈ AARP: 888 687 2277; www.aarp.org • Road Scholar: 617 426 7788; www.roadscholar.org

3 Disabled Travelers
Wheelchair-accessible entrances and restrooms are mandatory for public facilities built since 1987 – except for historic buildings and most B&Bs. For information on accessibility for disabled travelers, contact the Society for Accessible Travel and Hospitality (SATH). ◈ SATH: 212 447 7284 • www.sath.org

4 Gay Travelers
New England has several vibrant gay communities, including Provincetown on Cape Cod; Ogunquit, Maine; and Boston's South End. *Bay Windows*, New England's largest gay and lesbian weekly, includes arts and cultural listings for all six states.

5 Children
New England is a family-friendly place. Museums, zoos, and aquariums offer hands-on experiences for kids. Many restaurants offer children's menus. Most hotels or motels will supply an extra cot in a room for a modest fee. Some chain motels permit under-12s to stay free.

6 Hiking Holidays
Several companies arrange two- to five-day hiking excursions in the New England country-side. One of the best is New England Hiking Holidays. ◈ P.O. Box 1648, North Conway, NH 03860 • 603 356 9696 • www.nehikingholidays.com

7 Bicycling Holidays
Several outfitters organize multi-day group bicycling tours in some of the most scenic parts of Vermont and Maine. VBT, for example, even provides a "sag van" that gives exhausted riders a lift. ◈ 614 Monkton Rd, Bristol, VT 05443 • 800 245 3868 • www.vbt.com

8 Water-Sport Holidays
The Allagash Waterway undoubtedly provides the ultimate canoeing adventure in New England, while various outfitters will arrange Maine white-water river rafting *(for both, see pp56–7)*. Many expert sea kayakers tackle the popular Maine Island Trail from Portland to Machias on their own. Contact the Maine Island Trail Association for information. ◈ 58 Fore St., Portland, ME 04101 • 207 761 8225 • www.mita.org

9 Sporting Camps
Backwoods Maine has a long tradition of "sporting camps," often located many miles from civilization and accessible only by float plane. TV is unavailable and cell phones rarely work in these remote locations. Instead, campers can commune with nature by paddling, fishing, and hiking. ◈ Maine Sporting Camp Association, P.O. Box 119, Millinocket, ME 04462 • 207 723 6622 • www.mainesportingcamps.com

10 Windjammer Cruises
Sailing vacations, largely aboard schooner-rigged sailing vessels, are popular excursions on the Maine coast. Most of these give travelers the opportunity to participate in rigging and hauling sails *(see pp56–7)*.

 Same-sex marriages are legal in all New England states except Rhode Island and Maine.

Left **Crescent Beach State Park** Right **BosTix booth, Copley Square**

🔟 Budget Tips

1 Off-Season Travel
New England is busiest in summer, when children are out of school, and fall, when foliage is at its peak. Visiting in March or November can save you a bundle; hotels are empty, restaurants offer specials to lure diners, and air fares are lowest. Keep in mind, though, that attractions, chefs, and B&B operators often choose these slow times for their own vacations.

2 Discounts
Most museums and many attractions offer discounted admission to seniors (usually 65+) and students with proper ID. Many other discounts, including room rates, are available to members of the American Automobile Association (AAA) or its British affiliate, AA.

3 Free or Reduced Admissions
Most large museums offer reduced or free admission for one day, or part of one day, each week; check individual websites for details. Sometimes the free admission does not include special exhibitions or specific galleries.

4 Ticket Discounts
In Boston, BosTix kiosks (in Faneuil Hall Marketplace and Copley Square) sell half-price tickets to most non-commercial arts events and some commercial productions, from 10am on the day of the performance. Most purchases must be made with cash, but some are available on the website. 🔗 *www.bostix.com*

5 Free Outdoor Entertainment
Many cities and state parks throughout the region host free concerts and other entertainment, especially on summer weekends. In Boston, check the Thursday *G* section of the *Boston Globe* for films at the Hatch Shell, and for concerts on City Hall Plaza, Rowes Wharf, and Copley Square. Hampton Beach *(see p42)* has free concerts in July and August.

6 Outlet Shopping
To dispose of overstocks, leftover seasonal clothing, or goods that did not move at full price, many manufacturers of apparel and household goods maintain their own "outlet" stores; they are plentiful in Wrentham, Massachusetts; North Conway, New Hampshire; Freeport and Kittery, Maine; and Manchester, Vermont *(see pp62–3)*.

7 State Parks
State parks offer camping, picnicking, swimming, boating, hiking, and other outdoor activities for a relative pittance. (Some ocean-beach parking can be expensive, but that is an exception.) The states do not publish guides to their parks, but detailed information is available on their websites. 🔗 *CT: www.ct.gov/dep • MA: www.mass.gov/dcr/forparks.htm • ME: www.maine.gov/doc/parks/ • NH: www.nhparks.state.nh.us • RI: www.riparks.com • VT: www.vtstateparks.com*

8 Movie Matinees
In addition to giving senior discounts, most cinemas also discount tickets to first-run movies for afternoon screenings on weekdays, and sometimes for first screening of the day on weekends.

9 Weekday Fuel Purchases
Fuel prices are volatile. Stations offering the lowest typically raise the cost a few cents on Thursday then lower it again on Monday. Some offer substantial discounts for cash fuel purchases on Wednesday.

10 Cash Discounts
When dealing with small merchants (as opposed to chain stores), always ask if you can get a discount by paying cash. The answer is often yes, especially from antiques dealers. When you use a credit card, the merchant pays a percentage of the sale to the credit card company; most would rather give the money to you.

Left **Eggs Benedict** Center **Roadside diner sign** Right **The Clam Shack, Kennebunkport**

TOP 10 Eating and Drinking Tips

1 Dining Hours
Dining hours vary, but these are fairly average: breakfast, 5:30–10am; lunch, 11:30am–2pm; tea, 4–6pm; dinner, 5:30–10pm (though a limited bar menu may be available until midnight). Many restaurants and inns serve Sunday (and sometimes also Saturday) brunch, from late morning till early afternoon.

2 Reservations
For the best restaurants, reserve two weeks in advance. For the rest, reservations made the same day usually suffice. In a pinch, call at dinner time to see if there are any cancellations. Reservations are not necessary at most casual restaurants – indeed, many refuse to make them.

3 Lunch Bargains
Many New England restaurants offer smaller portions of their dinner items at lunch time, with correspondingly lower prices. During Boston Restaurant Weeks (third week of February, third week of August), many fine-dining establishments offer special two- and three-course lunches under $25. ✆ *www. restaurantweekboston.com*

4 Drinking Regulations
The legal minimum drinking age throughout New England is 21, and most everyone who looks 30 or younger will be asked for photo ID before being allowed to buy alcoholic drinks at a store, restaurant, or bar. Photo ID may be required to gain admission to a bar; assuming you do not have a driver's license from that state, your passport is usually the best form of ID. Drinking in public places is against the law, and penalties for drunken driving are severe, including fines, driving bans, and even jail time.

5 Brunch
The weekend brunch is popular in areas where people stay out late on Friday and Saturday nights – such as Boston's South End. This sort of brunch is usually an a la carte meal of large breakfast dishes, such as Eggs Benedict. The buffet brunch offered at many hotels tends to be more elaborate.

6 Roadside Diners
The roadside diner is making something of a comeback. Often only open for breakfast and lunch, they tend to specialize in egg dishes and grilled sandwiches. Some are open late at night to catch the hungry post-bar crowd.

7 Portion Size
European visitors are often amazed – and sometimes appalled – by US meal portions. Casual restaurants, in particular, tend to give exceedingly generous portions. It is common to take home a "doggie bag" of leftovers – in reality, the next day's lunch.

8 Street Food
In Boston you'll find street food vendors at Downtown Crossing, Faneuil Hall Marketplace, Copley Square, and along the Greenway Park in summer. Elsewhere in New England, look for food trucks at beaches and parks. The fare is usually simple hamburgers, hot dogs, wrap sandwiches, and burritos.

9 Chain Restaurants
Beyond the ubiquitous American fast-food chains, New England has some chains of its own, including Dunkin' Donuts (coffee and doughnuts), Au Bon Pain (croissants, pastries, coffee), and Boston Market (roast chicken). Legal Sea Foods has several locations in Massachusetts and one in Warwick, Rhode Island.

10 Seafood in the Rough
The best deals on fresh seafood – especially steamed lobster and clams – are generally at a "seafood in the rough" joint, of which the Maine lobster pound (*see p122*) is a specialized type. They are usually found at the shore, and feature a counter to place orders, and picnic tables for dining al fresco.

The first roadside diner – a converted horse-drawn freight wagon – appeared in Providence, Rhode Island, in 1872.

Left **Typical campground sign** Center **Sandy Neck Motel, Sandwich** Right **B&B sign**

🔟 Accommodation Tips

1 Types of Lodgings
Full-service hotels are rare in New England outside cities. Motels abound along highways; expect basic rooms with limited services. The true country inn is alive and well; they often feature a tavern or restaurant, with rooms on the upper levels. B&Bs also thrive – typically, they are large, often Victorian, private homes, with three to a dozen guest rooms and cheery, helpful host-owners.

2 Where to Base Yourself
Don't stay in the suburbs if you plan to visit Boston; and don't stay in Boston to visit the countryside – you'll waste all your time in coming and going. Distances are short in New England, but driving times can be deceptively long. If you want to cover a lot of ground, plan on moving every few days.

3 When to Book
For peak season (see p128), book as far ahead as you can; your lodging choices will be slim if you wait. During busy periods like Motorcycle Week in New Hampshire, the nearest lodging to the action may be 50 miles (80 km) away if you have not booked in advance.

4 B&B Inn Associations
Many B&B operators and innkeepers belong to the New England Innkeepers Association, which offers a directory of members at its website, but the most complete online listings are on the comm-ercial website Bed & Breakfasts Online. ✎ www.new englandinnsandresorts.com • www.bbonline.com

5 Traveling with Children
If you're traveling with small children, your most economical lodgings will be at motels – especially chain motels, where the usual bed configuration includes two double or queen-size beds per room, and perhaps a couch. Many motels will supply an extra cot for a modest fee. B&Bs often accept children only age 12 or older.

6 Campgrounds
The most economical camping is usually found in federal or state parks, and can be booked at the website of the National Recreation Reservation Service. Private camp-grounds can cost twice the price but provide a host of amenities. Many of the region's private campgrounds belong to the Northeast Camp-ground Association. ✎ www.recreation.gov • www.campnca.com

7 Chain Hotels and Motels
Hotel and motel chains are not known for their individuality; they thrive on providing a consistent, predictable product. But they often offer discounts for multiple bookings, and free nights through their loyalty programs. The major chains are: Days Inn; Hilton; Holiday Inn; Marriott; Motel 6; and Starwood.

8 Hidden Extras
Keep in mind that state and local lodging and sales taxes can add as much as 19 per cent to your bill; such charges are inescapable. Resorts typically charge 15 to 20 per cent either for staff gratuities or as a "resort fee" for facilities. Watch out for telephone charges; not only are long-distance calls billed at the highest rates, but you may be charged just for calling outside the hotel.

9 Minimum Stays
Many lodgings require a minimum stay of two or three nights during holiday periods, summer high season, or weekends during foliage season – unless rooms are still available at the last minute.

10 Accessibility
New England still has a long way to go with accessibility for wheelchair users. Many properties have only a few accessible rooms, and those sometimes lack roll-in, roll-out shower stalls. If you need a fully accessible room, ask before making a booking.

If you haven't reserved ahead, you can check with state visitor centers on interstate highways for lodging availability.

139

Left **Fairmont Copley Plaza Hotel** Right **Charles Hotel**

Boston Lodgings with Character

Liberty Hotel
Located at the foot of Beacon Hill, this swanky hotel incorporates the historic granite architecture of the Charles Street Jail with the latest in modern design. ✆ *215 Charles St., Boston, MA 02114 • Map V3 • 617 224 4000 • www.libertyhotel. com • $$$$$*

Fairmont Copley Plaza Hotel
All 383 rooms in this Edwardian *grande dame* on Copley Square in the heart of Back Bay have been renovated, updating the traditional genteel style of dark woods and rich fabrics. ✆ *138 St. James Ave., Boston, MA 02116 • Map U5 • 617 267 5300 • www.fairmont.com/ copleyplaza • $$$$$*

Back Bay Hotel
This limestone-faced boutique hotel was formerly the headquarters of the Boston Police, but nowadays its 225 rooms have feather pillows, duvets, and other comfort touches. It's superbly located within walking distance of South End restaurants, the Theater District, and Back Bay shopping. ✆ *350 Stuart St., Boston, MA 02116 • Map V4 • 617 266 7200 • www.doylecollection.com • $$$$$*

Kendall Hotel
This former firehouse recalls its firefighting days with historic memorabilia.

Eleven rooms occupy the former dormitory, while the remaining 66 are in a modern annex. The contemporary decor emphasizes Americana. ✆ *350 Main St., Cambridge, MA 02142 • Map T3 • 617 577 1300 • www.kendall hotel.com • $$$$*

Gryphon House
This townhouse built in the Richardsonian Romanesque style very much in vogue in 1895 has only eight spacious rooms, all with fireplace and wet bar. The quiet neighborhood is just steps from the campus of Boston University. Breakfast is included. ✆ *9 Bay State Rd., Boston, MA 02215 • Map S4 • 617 375 9003 • www. innboston.com • $$$$*

Charles Hotel
Recent renovation has preserved the Charles's hallmark style – a spare modernism softened by such homey touches as custom quilts on the beds. The hotel's plaza hosts a lively farmers' market and outdoor dining in summer. ✆ *1 Bennett St., Cambridge, MA 02138 • Map F2 • 617 864 1200 • www.charles hotel.com • $$$$$*

Beacon Hill Hotel & Bistro
This smart boutique lodging near Boston Common has the feel of a family-run Parisian hotel. Rooms are small but chic; sitting

room and private roof deck provide space to spread out. Breakfast is included. ✆ *25 Charles St., Boston, MA 02114 • Map V4 • 617 723 7575 • www. beaconhillhotel.com • $$$$$*

Charlesmark Hotel
Set in an 1892 townhouse, the Charlesmark resembles contemporary European urban boutique hotels, with its tiny lobby, compact rooms, and high-concept design. Breakfast is included. ✆ *655 Boylston St., Boston, MA 02116 • Map U5 • 617 247 1212 • http://charles markhotel.com • $$$*

Boston Park Plaza Hotel & Towers
With its glamorous lobby and 941 rooms (some of them admittedly small), the Park Plaza has an edge over other large Boston hotels. Simple but pleasing modern decor; convenient location between Back Bay and the Theater District; bargain rooms often available. ✆ *50 Park Plaza at Arlington St., Boston, MA 02116 • Map V4 • 617 426 2000 • www.bostonpark plaza.com • $$$$*

Harborside Inn
Housed in a granite former spice warehouse, this boutique hotel is located steps from Faneuil Hall Marketplace. ✆ *185 State St., Boston, MA 02109 • Map X3 • 617 723 7500 • www.harborsideinn boston.com • $$$$$*

Even Boston's priciest hotels run specials, or drop their rates in slow periods like January, March, and November. Always inquire.

Price Categories

For a standard, double room per night (with breakfast if included), taxes and extra charges.	**$** under $125
	$$ $125–175
	$$$ $175–225
	$$$$ $225–300
	$$$$$ over $300

Left **The Study at Yale** Right **Hawthorne Hotel, lobby**

🔟 In-Town Hotels

Hotel Providence
Though Providence has a wealth of boutique hotels, this luxurious yet unpretentious downtown spot mixes traditional formality with contemporary design. 🕲 *311 Westminster St., Providence, RI 02903 • Map E4 • 401 861 8000 • www.the hotelprovidence.com • $$$$*

Portland Harbor Hotel
The decor of this comfortable business and leisure property on the edge of the Old Port is cheery yet modern. For maximum tranquillity, ask for a room overlooking the garden courtyard. 🕲 *468 Fore St., Portland, ME 04101 • Map N4 • 207 775 9090 • www.portland harborhotel.com • $$$$$*

The Study at Yale
Facing the Yale School of Art in the midst of Yale's most striking modern architecture, The Study is almost self-consciously sleek and up-to-date, with flat-screen TV, free Wi-Fi access, and iPod docking station on the clock radio. 🕲 *1157 Chapel St., New Haven, CT 06511 • Map C5 • 203 503 3900 • www. studyhotels.com • $$$$*

Sheraton Portsmouth Harborside Hotel
Two blocks from Market Square and next to the whale-watch and harbor cruise docks, this modern business hotel is equally well suited to the leisure traveler. Redwood sauna, large pool, and extensive fitness room set it apart from other Portsmouth lodgings. 🕲 *250 Market St., Portsmouth, NH 03801 • Map N6 • 603 431 2300 • www.sheraton portsmouth.com • $$$$*

Hawthorne Hotel
Built in 1925 in the Federal style of a century earlier, the Hawthorne sits near Salem Common and the Peabody Essex Museum *(see p45)*. While the decor is American traditional verging on Colonial, the hotel also offers free Wi-Fi. 🕲 *18 Washington Sq., Salem, MA 01970 • Map F2 • 978 744 4080 • www.hawthorne hotel.com • $$$*

The Latchis Hotel & Theatre
The Latchis is one of only two remaining Art Deco buildings in Vermont. It has modest rooms, free Wi-Fi, and a three-screen theater showing art and independent films. 🕲 *50 Main St., Brattleboro, VT 05301 • Map K6 • 802 254 6300 • www.latchis.com • $$*

Providence Biltmore
This 1922 downtown mini-skyscraper was completely renovated to create smartly appointed rooms in contemporary style with comfortable beds, heavy draperies, and deluxe linens. Regular rooms tend to be small, making junior suites a better bet for longer stays. 🕲 *11 Dorrance St., Providence, RI 02903 • Map E4 • 401 421 0700 • www.providencebiltmore. com • $$$$*

Hilton Burlington
Burlington's most upscale hotel sits between the heart of downtown and the shore of Lake Champlain. The best rooms have breathtaking views of the lake, with the Adirondack Mountains rising behind. 🕲 *60 Battery St., Burlington, VT 05401 • Map J3 • 802 658 6500 • www.1hilton. com • $$$$*

Lane Hotel
In this lushly appointed traditional hotel on the broad Main Street of this college town, every one of the 40 rooms is different. Great off-season discounts. 🕲 *30 Main St., Keene, NH 03431 • Map L6 • 603 357 7070 • www.thelanehotel.com • $$$$*

Forty 1° North
Spacious and stylish, this contemporary resort offers immersion in the downtown Newport scene, along with its own marina and piers on the famous yachting harbor. Casual luxury is augmented by high-tech amenities. 🕲 *351 Thames St., Newport, RI 02840 • Map F5 • 401 846 8018 • www.41north.com • $$$$$*

These city hotels are popular venues for weddings and other celebrations. Ask for a room away from function areas.

Left **Red Lion Inn** Center **Governor Bradford Country House Inn** Right **Deerfield Inn**

TOP 10 Country Inns (Southern)

1 Red Lion Inn
The Red Lion has been welcoming travelers since just before the American Revolution, though the current main inn (there are several guest houses too) is a commodious Victorian structure with a perfect porch for sitting and rocking. Breakfast is extra. ✎ *30 Main St., Stockbridge, MA 01262 • Map B3 • 413 298 5545 • www.redlioninn. com • $$$$$*

2 Old Inn on the Green
The spacious rooms of this circa-1800 inn with adjacent guest house on the picturesque green of this Berkshires village are decorated with country antiques, quilts, and folk art. ✎ *134 Hartsville-New Marlborough Rd., New Marlborough, MA 01230 • Map B3 • www.oldinn.com • $$$$*

3 Warfield House Inn
Fall foliage season brings dramatic views of the vast property. Rooms are in two farmhouses, most with a large, wood-burning fireplace in the living room. ✎ *200 Warfield Rd., Charlemont, MA 01339 • Map C2 • 413 339 6600 • www.warfield houseinn.com • $*

4 Deerfield Inn
Built in 1884, this country inn sits in the heart of 350-year-old Deerfield. The 24 restful rooms are all different shapes and sizes, but are consistently decorated in American Colonial Revival style. Historic Deerfield's museum store is on the premises. ✎ *81 Main St., Deerfield, MA 01342 • Map C2 • 413 774 5587 • www. deerfieldinn.com • $$$$*

5 Longfellow's Wayside Inn
The oldest operating inn in the US (since 1716), The Wayside was made famous by Henry Wadsworth Longfellow's *Tales of a Wayside Inn.* The bar and dining rooms ooze antique charm, but the plumbing is up to date. ✎ *72 Wayside Inn Rd., Sudbury, MA 01776 • Map E2 • 978 443 1776 • www.wayside.org • $$$*

6 The Griswold Inn
An Essex fixture since 1801, the "Gris" reflects in its decor the maritime history of this important Connecticut River port town. Five dining rooms dominate the historic structure, leaving guests to occupy the common rooms at Hayden House next door. Breakfast extra. ✎ *36 Main St., Essex, CT 06426 • Map D5 • 860 767 1776 • www.griswoldinn.com • $$$*

7 Wake Robin Inn
A former girls' school that exudes country charm, the main inn (open all year) holds 23 rooms with traditional decor. A summer motel adds 15 more. A walking trail through the large property passes the wild trilliums (also known as wake robins), for which the inn is named. ✎ *106 Sharon Rd., Rte. 41, Lakeville, CT 06039 • Map B4 • 860 435 2000 • www. wakerobin inn.com • $$*

8 Fife 'n Drum
Eight rooms with vaulted ceilings occupy the main inn next to the Fife 'n Drum restaurant; there are three more in an adjacent Victorian house. Well-placed for Kent's up-scale boutiques, galleries, crafts stores, and ace chocolatier. ✎ *53 N. Main St., Kent, CT 06757 • Map B4 • 860 927 3509 • www. fifendrum.com • $$$*

9 The Inn at Woodstock Hill
The steeply-pitched hip roof, multiple dormers, and white clapboard siding make this 1816 inn a visual emblem of rural New England. All rooms have private baths. ✎ *94 Plaine Hill Rd., Woodstock, CT 06281 • Map D4 • 860 928 0528 • www. woodstockhill.net • $$$*

10 Governor Bradford Country House Inn
The 1745 grand mansion of historic landmark Mount Hope Farm lets you feel like a true country squire. ✎ *250 Metacom Ave., Rte. 136, Bristol, RI 02809 • Map F4 • 401 254 9300 • www. mounthopefarm.com • $$$$*

Inn at Shelburne Farms

Price Categories		
For a standard, double room per night (with breakfast if included), taxes and extra charges.	**$** under $125
	$$ $125–175
	$$$ $175–225
	$$$$ $225–300
	$$$$$ over $300

🔟 Country Inns (Northern)

1 Inn at Shelburne Farms

This late-19th-century mansion overlooking Lake Champlain is the centerpiece of a historic park (see p103). The grounds were designed by Frederick Law Olmsted, known as the father of US landscape architecture. 🏵 1611 Harbor Rd., Shelburne, VT 05482 • Map J3 • 802 985 8498 • www.shelburnefarms.org • $$$$$

2 Inn at Weston

A romantic hideaway in a charming village surrounded by ski mountains, the inn – dotted with orchids from the innkeeper's greenhouse – often hosts small weddings and civil unions. Nine rooms have fireplaces, some have double whirlpool tubs. 🏵 630 Main St., Rte. 100, Weston, VT 05161 • Map K5 • 802 824 6789 • www.innweston.com • $$$$

3 Four Chimneys Inn

This handsome white clapboard inn (with four chimneys, of course) has just 11 rooms, whose old-fashioned grandeur and contemporary amenities make it a cozy retreat in historic Bennington. 🏵 21 West Rd., Old Bennington, VT 05201 • Map J6 • 802 447 3500 • www.fourchimneys.com • $$$

4 Swift House Inn

The rooms are spread across the Federal-era main house, a modernized carriage house, and a small gate-house on a hill above the picturesque college town. Some rooms have fireplaces and whirlpool tubs. Breakfasts are generous. 🏵 25 Stewart Ln., Middlebury, VT 05753 • Map J4 • 802 388 9925 • www.swifthouseinn.com • $$$

5 Quechee Inn at Marshland Farm

A spectacular setting across the road from the Quechee River makes this 1793 property a true country idyll. The rooms feel like spare bedrooms at grandma's house, but the comfortable rustic lounge has a welcoming fireplace. 🏵 1119 Quechee Main St., Quechee, VT 05059 • Map K5 • 802 295 3133 • www.quecheeinn.com • $$$

6 Pitcher Inn

Whimsical themed decor in 11 rooms has won this luxury property features in practically every design magazine. The Trout Room has a bed of real tree trunks, and a river-stone fireplace. 🏵 275 Main St., Warren, VT 05674 • Map K4 • 802 496 6350 • www.pitcherinn.com • $$$$$

7 Newcastle Inn

Overlooking the Damariscotta River harbor, this country inn is perfectly situated for exploring the midcoast Maine peninsulas. Rooms are spread among main inn, cottage, and former carriage house; some have fireplaces. There's a guests-only pub, as well. 🏵 60 River Rd., Newcastle, ME 04553 • Map P4 • 207 563 5685 • www.newcastleinn.com • $$$

8 Adair Country Inn

Each room in this romantic inn, set on a historic estate, is named after a nearby peak of the White Mountains. Great for watching wildlife and enjoying the alpine landscape. 🏵 80 Guider Lane, Bethlehem, NH 03574 • Map L3 • 603 444 2600 • www.adairinn.com • $$$$$

9 New London Inn

This Federal-style 1792 inn has been transformed into a chic retreat with boldly artistic rooms. The owners wisely maintained the country-hotel look in the public areas, including the double-decker porch with wicker chairs and rockers. 🏵 353 Main St., New London, NH 03257 • Map L5 • 603 526 2791 • www.newlondoninn.net • $$$

10 The Hancock Inn

This wonderfully antique hostelry in the Monadnock foothills has been operated continuously since 1789. The floorboards creak winsomely, but all rooms have modern facilities. 🏵 33 Main St., Hancock, NH 03449 • Map L6 • 603 525 3318 • www.hancockinn.com • $$$$

Left **Mill Falls, Bay Point** Right **Basin Harbor Club**

TOP 10 Lakeside Lodgings

1 The WilloughVale Inn on Lake Willoughby

This dog-friendly inn with eight additional lakeside (or lakeview) cottages overlooks a long finger of lake surrounded by mountains. Some cabins are rustic; inn rooms are perfect for the genteel fisherman. ✪ Rte. 5A S., Westmore, VT 05860 • Map L2 • 802 525 4123 • www. willoughvale.com • $$$

2 Inn at Smith Cove

This Victorian inn with long porches and a delightful gazebo on the dock sits on a quiet corner of Lake Winnipesaukee. The quirky tower suite has bedroom, sitting room, and whirlpool tub. ✪ 19 Roberts Rd., Gilford, NH 03249 • Map M5 • 603 293 1111 • www.innatsmith cove.com • $$

3 Inns & Spa at Mill Falls

The spacious rooms of this tastefully restrained inn in a luxury complex adjacent to a restored linen mill are furnished in English country style. There's an indoor pool, and sauna. No breakfast. ✪ 312 Daniel Webster Hwy., Meredith, NH • Map M5 • 603 279 7006 • www. millfalls.com • $$$$

4 Purity Spring Resort

Loons aren't the only repeat visitors to Purity Lake; families come back year after year to this rustic resort founded in the 19th century. In summer they paddle, in winter they ski. Rates generally include three meals daily. ✪ 1251 Eaton Rd., Rte. 153, East Madison, NH 03849 • Map M4 • 603 367 8896 • www. purityspring.com • $$$$

5 Inn on Newfound Lake

This country stagecoach inn on the Boston to Montreal route has welcomed guests since 1840. Renovation has created an upscale Victorian showpiece. ✪ 1030 Mayhew Tpke., Rte. 3A, Bridgewater, NH 03222 • Map L5 • 603 744 9111 • www.newfound lake.com • $$$

6 Hopkins Inn

A favorite escape for city folks since 1847, this inn on a knoll overlooking the north shore of Lake Waramaug adjoins the superb Hopkins Vineyard. Winter cross-country skiing rivals the pleasures of summer lakeside idling. ✪ 22 Hopkins Rd., New Preston, CT 06777 • Map B4 • 860 868 7295 • www. thehopkinsinn.com • $$

7 Inn at Long Lake

This handsome Victorian inn with 16 antiques-packed yet unfussy rooms makes a spectacular base for western-Maine fall foliage. ✪ 15 Lake House Rd., Naples, ME 04055 • Map N4 • 207 693 6226 • www. innatlonglake.com • $$$

8 Kineo View Motor Lodge

So sensational are the views to be had from this family-run three-story motel on a long hill above Moosehead Lake that travelers often pull in for photos. Most rooms have two double beds; all have balconies for mountain and lake views. Continental breakfast summer and fall only. ✪ Rte. 15, Greenville, ME 04441 • Map P1 • 207 695 4470, 800 659 8439 • www. kineoview.com • $

9 Lake Motel

The budget choice in expensive Wolfeboro, this traditional motel with clean, spacious rooms and lovely lawn has its own lakeside beaches. It's a five-minute stroll to Wolfeboro harbor on Lake Winnipesaukee. No breakfast. ✪ Rte. 28, Wolfeboro, NH 03894 • Map M5 • 603 569 1110 • May–Oct • www. thelakemotel.com • $$

10 Basin Harbor Club

Whether you take one of 74 cabins or book a room in the guest houses, you'll join a resort community at Basin Harbor. Sailing and waterskiing on Lake Champlain (lessons are available) are big summer hits. The rate includes all meals in summer. ✪ 4800 Basin Harbor Rd., Vergennes, VT 05491 • Map J4 • 802 475 2311 • www. basinharbor.com • $$$$$

Price Categories

For a standard,		
double room per	**$**	under $125
night (with breakfast	**$$**	$125–175
if included), taxes	**$$$**	$175–225
and extra charges.	**$$$$**	$225–300
	$$$$$	over $300

Left **Edgewater Motor Inn** Right **Fisherman's Wharf Inn**

🔟 Coastal Lodgings

1 Atlantic Oceanside
Set near the entrance to Acadia National Park *(see pp10–11)*, the 12-acre former estate of Klondike billionaire Sir Harry Oakes holds a 153-room resort with jaw-dropping vistas, as well as indoor and outdoor swimming pools. Breakfast is extra in summer. 🏛 *119 Eden St., Rte. 3, Bar Harbor, ME 04609 • Map R3 • 207 288 5801 • www.barharbor.com • $$$$*

2 Spouter Inn
Just across the street from Lincolnville Beach and its lobster pound, this 1832 house transformed into an inn by the current owner's parents strikes a perfect balance between country farmhouse and nautical getaway. 🏛 *2506 Rte. 1, Lincolnville Beach, ME • Map Q3 • 207 789 5171 • www.spouterinn.com • $$$*

3 Captain Fairfield Inn
This old Federal mansion captures the grace of a bygone era. The bedrooms range from traditional decor to soft-edged modern comfort. 🏛 *8 Pleasant St., Kennebunkport, ME 04046 • Map N5 • 207 967 4454 • www.captainfairfield.com • $$$$*

4 Edgewater Motor Inn
Just five blocks west of the pier at Old Orchard Beach *(see p120)*, this fabulously updated motel with a wide variety of rooms in different sizes and bedding configurations stays open all year. No breakfast. 🏛 *57 West Grand Ave., Old Orchard Beach, ME 04064 • Map N5 • 207 934 2221 • www.theedgewatermotorinn.com • $$$$*

5 Fisherman's Wharf Inn
Rooms are large, comfortable, and unpretentious, every one with its own private balcony overlooking the harbor. Breakfast extra. 🏛 *22 Commercial St., Pier 6, Boothbay Harbor, ME 04538 • Map P4 • 207 633 5090 • May–Oct • www.fishermanswharfinn.com • $$*

6 Inn at Castle Hill
Understated elegance and serenity characterize this tranquil inn on the Crane Estate. Walk to extraordinary Crane Beach *(see p42)* backed by rolling sand dunes. 🏛 *280 Argilla Rd., Ipswich, MA 01938 • Map F2 • 978 412 2555 • www.theinnatcastlehill.com • $$$*

7 Hyatt Regency Newport
Set on Goat Island in Narragansett Bay, this luxurious resort hotel is a quick boat ride from the Newport hubbub. The outdoor saltwater pool and long, green lawns invite lounging. 🏛 *1 Goat Island, Newport, RI 02840 • Map F5 • 401 851 1234 • www.newport.hyatt.com • $$$$$*

8 Wellfleet Motel and Lodge
Its location at the north end of the Cape Cod Rail Trail and across Rte. 6 from the Audubon wildlife sanctuary is key, but so is the hospitality at this hybrid property of motel and lodge rooms. Many of the rooms have private balconies or patios overlooking a landscaped courtyard. Breakfast is extra. 🏛 *170 Rte. 6, S. Wellfleet, MA 02663 • Map H4 • 508 349 3535 • late Apr–early Nov • www.wellfleetmotel.com • $$*

9 The Isaiah Clark House
This authentic sea captain's saltbox, built in 1785, expanded in 1835, and converted to an inn in 1985, sits less than a mile from Paine's Beach, one of the best swimming holes on Cape Cod Bay. Comfortable and elegant furnishings. 🏛 *1187 Main St., Rte. 6A, Brewster, MA 02631 • Map H4 • 508 896 2223 • Apr–Nov • www.isaiahclark.com • $$$*

10 Steamboat Inn
With each room named for a vessel from Mystic's sailing heyday, this quirkily designed riverside inn by the celebrated drawbridge is as nautical as it gets. Evening sherry and cookies are served. 🏛 *73 Steamboat Wharf, Mystic, CT 06355 • Map D5 • 860 536 8300 • www.steamboatinnmystic.com • $$$$*

Left **The Basalms** Right **Trapp Family Lodge**

Ski Country Lodgings

The Balsams
Its magical setting on a lake surrounded by mountains makes this venerable north-country resort postcard-perfect; come here in summer for some of the best golf, and in winter for some of the best skiing in New England. ✪ *Rte. 26, Dixville Notch, NH 03576 • Map M2 • 603 255 3400 • www. thebalsams.com • $$$$*

Alpenrose Motel
On the mountain road almost exactly halfway between the village and the ski slopes, the Alpenrose has spacious rooms and features useful boot- and glove-dryers. Some two-room units will sleep up to five, and two of the nine rooms are pet-friendly. ✪ *2619 Mountain Rd., Stowe, Vt 05672 • Map K3 • 802 253 7277 • www. gostowe.com • $$$*

Mountain View Grand Resort & Spa
This venerable hotel earns its name with stunning mountain views in two directions. It's perfect for both day hikers and alpine skiers. ✪ *Mountain View Rd., Whitefield, NH 03598 • Map M3 • 866 484 3843 • www.mountainviewgrand. com • $$$$*

Sunset Hill House
This country inn and adjacent farmhouse sit right outside Franconia Notch State Park. With its Victorian decor, it's a genteel base for winter activities in the White Mountains. ✪ *231 Sunset Hill Rd., Sugar Hill, NH • Map L3 • 603 823 5522 • www.sunsethillhouse. com • $$$*

Trapp Family Lodge
This world-famous resort on the vast property of the family that inspired *The Sound of Music* has a large Austrian-style main lodge and 100 guest houses. The cross-country ski trail is among the best in the US. Breakfast extra. ✪ *700 Trapp Hill Rd., Stowe, VT 05672 • Map K3 • 802 253 8511 • www. trappfamily.com • $$$$*

Craftsbury Outdoor Center
Rustic cabins and simply furnished but comfortable rooms, some with shared baths, are a perfect fit in any season at the capital of Nordic skiing in Vermont. All rates include three acclaimed meals daily. ✪ *535 Lost Nation Rd., Craftsbury Common, VT 05827 • Map K2 • 802 586 7767 • www.craftsbury. com • $–$$$$*

Red Clover Inn
This farm-based inn near Pico Peak is a well-kept secret among skiers. Rooms are tranquil and cozy in the main inn, huge and comfy in the carriage-house. ✪ *7 Woodward Rd., Mendon, VT 05701 • Map K5 • 802 775 2290 • www. redcloverinn.com • $$$$*

Bethel Inn
Not far from Sunday River ski resort, this property includes a main inn (a cluster of four Colonial-style buildings), some townhouses, and a championship golf course. Rates include golf and dinner in summer; cross-country trail fees in winter. ✪ *On the Common, Bethel, ME 04217 • Map N3 • 207 824 2175 • www. bethelinn.com • $$$*

Rangeley Inn
The main inn is a meticulously restored country hotel. Rooms in the adjacent motel cost roughly the same and have porches overlooking the lake. It's a popular winter destination for skiing at Saddleback. The public beach nearby offers summer boating and swimming. ✪ *2443 Main St., Rangeley, ME • Map N2 • 207 864 3341 • closed Apr–May • www. rangeleyinn.com • $$*

Inn at Sawmill Farm
The inn is just up the road from the Mount Snow ski area, but even in winter the decor makes everything feel warm and cheery. The stylishly appointed rooms are generously sized for a historic inn. The rest-aurant is superb *(see p105)*. ✪ *Crosstown Rd., West Dover, VT 05356 • Map K6 • 802 464 8131 • www.theinnatsawmillfarm. com • $$$$*

Island Inn

Price Categories

For a standard, double room per night (with breakfast if included), taxes and extra charges.

$	under $125
$$	$125–175
$$$	$175–225
$$$$	$225–300
$$$$$	over $300

🔟 Island Getaways

1 Island Inn
This modernized 1816 inn right above the ferry landing has some of the best views on Monhegan. Half the 34 rooms and suites have private baths but there's no TV or room phones, and cellphone coverage is poor – which just makes Monhegan more of a getaway than ever. ◎ *Monhegan Island, ME 04852 • Map Q4 • 207 596 0371 • late May–mid-Oct • www.islandinn monhegan.com • $$$$*

2 Inn on Peaks Island
Just a 20-minute ferry ride from the Portland waterfront, this in-harbor getaway lets you look back on the mainland with superiority from your private deck with skyline views of Portland. Hideaway rooms include whirlpool tubs and cozy fireplaces. No breakfast. ◎ *33 Island Ave., Peaks Island, ME 04108 • Map P4 • 207 766 5100 • www. innonpeaks.com • $$$$$*

3 The Nashua House Hotel
Many of the bedrooms in this charming Victorian inn in the center of Oak Bluffs village have ocean views. It's a Vineyard rarity, open all year for winter escapes. Rooms share baths. Breakfast extra. ◎ *30 Kennebec Ave., Oak Bluffs, Martha's Vineyard, MA 02557 • Map G5 • 508 693 0043 • www. nashuahouse.com • $$$*

4 Edgartown Inn
With its white clapboards, cedar shingles, and large front porch, this 1798 sea captain's home is an iconic example of Edgartown architecture. For greater seclusion, opt for a garden-house room. Breakfast extra. ◎ *56 North Water St., Edgartown, Martha's Vineyard, MA 02539 • Map G5 • 508 627 4794 • Apr–Oct • www. edgartowninn.com • $$$*

5 Cliff Lodge
The 12 airy rooms in this 1771 whalemaster's eyrie above Nantucket Harbor embody a style that's half Old Nantucket, half Ralph Lauren (who modeled a decor line on the local style). ◎ *9 Cliff Rd., Nantucket, MA 02554 • Map H5 • 508 228 9480 • www.clifflodgenantucket. com • $$$$*

6 The Wauwinet
Set at the east end of Nantucket Harbor, the Wauwinet offers an escape from the bustle of the village into luxurious lodgings in Nantucket's natural wilds. Breakfast extra. ◎ *120 Wauwinet Rd., Nantucket, MA 02584 • Map H5 • 508 228 0145 • May–Oct • www. wauwinet.com • $$$$$*

7 White Elephant
This tasteful new-construction hotel stakes out the most desirable patch of waterfront in Nantucket village. Most rooms have fireplaces and harbor views; 11 garden cottages provide more space and privacy. Breakfast extra. ◎ *Easton St., Nantucket, MA 02554 • Map H5 • 508 228 2500 • Apr–Dec • www.white elephanthotel.com • $$$$$*

8 National Hotel
The grand 45-room National is only steps from the ferry landing. In classic resort-hotel fashion, a covered porch with rockers runs the length of the building. Standard rooms are small, but all have private baths. Breakfast extra. ◎ *Water St., Block Island, RI 02807 • Map E6 • 401 466 2901 • May–Oct • www.block islandhotels.com • $$$$$*

9 Atlantic Inn
This 22-room Victorian inn with acclaimed restaurant is across the street from Block Island's best bathing beach. The expansive hillside property is dotted with stunning gardens. ◎ *High St., Old Harbor, Block Island • Map E6 • 401 466 5883 • late Apr–Oct • www.atlanticinn. com • $$$$*

10 Shore Acres
Watch the sun rise through morning mist on Lake Champlain from one of 19 lakeside rooms or four garden-house rooms a short walk away. Breakfast offered in Fall only. ◎ *237 Shore Acres Dr., North Hero Island, VT • Map J2 • 802 372 8722 • www. shoreacres.com • $$$*

Left **Mount Washington Hotel and golf course** Right **Woodstock Inn and Resort**

TOP 10 Resorts

1 Mount Washington Hotel & Resort

This palatial hotel offers upcountry elegance in a dramatic natural setting. In summer, golf is the lure; in winter, skiing and dogsledding. The most popular package includes breakfast and dinner at any of the resort's five restaurants. ✪ *Rte. 302, Bretton Woods, NH 03575 • Map M3 • 603 278 1000 • www.mountwashington resort.com • \$\$\$\$\$*

2 Woodstock Inn & Resort

The Rockefellers built this huge modern pile to look as if it had been on the town green for centuries. Rooms have every conceivable comfort, but you'll find it hard to leave the lobby with its massive fieldstone fireplace. ✪ *14 The Green, Woodstock, VT 05091 • Map K5 • 802 457 1100 • www.woodstockinn. com • \$\$\$\$\$*

3 Cranwell Resort, Spa & Golf Club

Set in a gilded-age Berkshires country estate, this resort offers extensive spa facilities, an Olympic-size indoor pool, and an 18-hole championship golf course. ✪ *55 Lee Rd., Lenox, MA 01240 • Map B3 • 413 637 1364 • www.cranwell.com • \$\$\$\$\$*

4 Foxwoods Resort Casino

The most successful casino complex in North America, Foxwoods has three of its own hotels and accommodations at MGM Grand. Two Trees Inn, a 3-minute shuttle ride from gaming tables, is the best buy. Rooms closer to the action are more expensive. ✪ *Rte. 2, Ledyard, CT 06339 • Map D5 • 800 FOXWOOD • www.foxwoods.com • \$\$\$\$*

5 Castle Hill Inn & Resort

Exclusive Newport's most exclusive resort, Castle Hill occupies a huge green clifftop peninsula. The main mansion was the summer home of scientist and explorer Alexander Agassiz. ✪ *590 Ocean Dr., Newport, RI 02840 • Map F5 • 401 849 3800 • www. castlehill inn.com • \$\$\$\$\$*

6 Chatham Bars Inn

This luxurious 1914 resort at the elbow of Cape Cod has an exquisite private sand beach. Newer accommodations in cottages or adjacent to the spa are even larger and more luxurious. ✪ *297 Shore Rd., Chatham, MA 02633 • Map H4 • 508 945 0096 • www.chatham barsinn.com • \$\$\$\$\$*

7 Cliff House Resort & Spa

Set atop Bald Head Cliff, the rooms at this iconic oceanside resort (since 1872) all have balconies for sweeping vistas. ✪ *Shore Rd., Ogunquit, ME 03907 • Map N5 • 207 361 1000 • Apr–mid-Dec • www. cliffhousemaine.com • \$\$\$\$*

8 Equinox Resort & Spa

Spacious, country-style rooms dot four buildings of this 18th-century resort with amazing mountain views. Outdoor activities on offer include boating, falconry, golf, flyfishing, shooting, winter snowmobiling, and skiing. ✪ *3567 Main St., Rte. 7A, Manchester, VT 05254 • Map K6 • 802 362 4700 • www.equinoxresort.com • \$\$\$\$\$*

9 Stoweflake Mountain Resort & Spa

Located halfway up the access highway to the ski-and-hiking Mecca of Mt. Mansfield *(see p54)*, Stoweflake is the luxury choice in sports-crazed Stowe. Choose from gracious modern hotel or A-frame townhouses. ✪ *1746 Mountain Rd., Stowe, VT 05672 • Map K3 • 802 253 7355 • www. stoweflake.com • \$\$\$\$\$*

10 The Birches Resort

Choose your accommodations from rustic waterfront cabin, small home, tentlike cabin, wilderness yurt, or old-fashioned lodge. The resort is geared to guests who love fishing, hiking, paddling, snowmobiling, and other woodsy pursuits. Breakfast included in some seasons. ✪ *Rtes. 6/15, Rockwood, ME 04478 • Map Q5 • 207 534 7305 • www.birches.com • \$\$*

Most resorts charge a resort facilities fee on top of the room rate.

Price Categories

For a standard, double room per night (with breakfast if included), taxes and extra charges.	**$** under $125
	$$ $125–175
	$$$ $175–225
	$$$$ $225–300
	$$$$$ over $300

The Inn at Long Trail

Budget-Friendly Lodgings

Curtis House Inn
This mid-18th-century lodging retains its quirky style without benefit of a designer makeover, even in upscale Woodbury. Some rooms are small or share baths. ◈ 506 Main St. S., Woodbury, CT 06798 • Map B5 • 203 263 2101 • www.curtishouseinn.com • $

Monhegan House
Almost nothing has changed about this island guest house since artists began flocking to Monhegan Island (see p40) a century ago. In decor, the 28 rooms are "contemporary country chic" – but they've always been that way. ◈ Main Rd., Monhegan Island, ME 04852 • Map Q4 • 207 594 7983 • late May–early Oct • www.monheganhouse. com • $$

East Wind Inn
Wake to lobster boats heading out to haul their catch at this sprawling harborfront inn. Rooms are furnished with a mix of country furniture and local antiques. Some of the 26 rooms share baths. ◈ Mechanic St., Tenants Harbor, ME 04860 • Map Q4 • 207 372 6366 • May–Oct • www.east windinn.com • $$$

Colonial Gables Oceanfront Village
Small cottages, many freshly renovated, dot a hillside sloping down to a private beach on Penobscot Bay. The cottages have their own kitchens and front porches. The property also has 13 motel rooms. ◈ 7 Eagle Lane, Belfast, ME 04915 • Map Q3 • 207 338 4000 • May–Oct • www. colonialgables.com • $$

Herbert Grand Hotel
Step back to 1917 at this marvelously old-fashioned mountain hotel close to Sugarloaf skiing and golf. Rooms are small, but all have baths. The terrace over the portico serves as evening social center. ◈ 246 Main St., Kingfield, ME 04947 • Map N2 • 207 265 2000 • www. herbertgrandhotel.com • $

Kancamagus Swift River Inn
One of the rare lodgings on the Kancamagus Highway (see p36), this modest inn has 10 spacious, comfortable rooms with eclectic decor. North Conway shopping and White Mountain National Forest trails are nearby. ◈ 1316 Kancamagus Hwy., Albany, NH 03818 • Map M4 • 603 447 2332 • www. swiftriverinn.com • $

The Inn at Long Trail
Hikers adore this rustic lodge at the intersection of the Appalachian and Long trails in the heart of the Green Mountains. (There's a mail drop for through-hikers.) Vermont skiers also flock here. There's an Irish pub on the premises (see p104). ◈ 709 Rte. 4, Sherburne Pass, Killington, VT 05751 • Map K5 • 802 775 7181 • Jun–Apr • www.innatlong trail.com • $$$

Breezeway Resort
Misquamicut Beach (see p42) is a short walk from this family-friendly motel and apartment complex where every room has at least a refrigerator and some have cooking facilities. ◈ 70 Winnapaug Rd., Misquamicut, RI 02891 • Map E5 • 401 348 8953 • May–mid-Oct • www. breezewayresort.com • $$$

Sandy Neck Motel
This charming and well-kept older motel is located at the entrance to the extensive sand bar of Sandy Neck Beach, near the tidal marshes famous for birding. No breakfast. ◈ 669 Rte. 6A, Sandwich, MA 02537 • Map G4 • 508 362 3992 • Apr–Oct • www. sandyneck.com • $$

Days Inn
This well-maintained chain motel with spacious rooms is right at the southern edge of town. It's great value for money, and makes an excellent base for foraging for antiques in nearby Sheffield and South Egremont. ◈ 372 Main St., Great Barrington, MA 01230 • Map B3 • 413 528 3150 • www.daysinn.com • $

General Index

Page numbers in **bold** type refer to main entries.

Index

Acknowledgements

The Authors

Between them, Patricia Harris and David Lyon have experienced New England from the ground up, working such varied jobs as a commercial fisherman, travel tour leader, arts administrator, and restaurant line cook. They have lived in four New England states and traveled relentlessly in all six.
In addition to co-authoring more than two dozen books, they write about travel, food, fine arts, and popular culture for magazines, newspapers, and websites, including HungryTravelers.com. They co-wrote DK's *Eyewitness Travel Guide to Boston* and *Top 10 Boston*.

Produced by Coppermill Books, 55 Salop Road, London E17 7HS
Editorial Director Chris Barstow
Designer Ian Midson
Factchecker Julie Dalton
Proofreader Huw Hennessy
Indexer Helen Peters

Main Photographer Tony Souter
Additional Photography
Alan Briere, Demetrio Carrasco, Ed Homonylo, Philip C. Jackson, Patricia Harris, David Lyons, Rough Guides/ Angus Oborn, Linda Whitwam
Maps by Simonetta Giori, Dominic Beddow (Draughtsman Ltd)

FOR DORLING KINDERSLEY
Publisher Douglas Amrine
List Manager Christine Stroyan
Managing Art Editors Sunita Gahir, Mabel Chan
Senior Editor Sadie Smith
Project Designer Tracy Smith
Senior Cartographic Editor Casper Morris
Picture Researchers Ellen Root, Rhiannon Furbear
DTP Jason Little
Production Controller Rita Sinha

Additional Design and Editorial Assistance

Caroline Elliker, Fay Franklin, Camilla Gersh, Lydia Halliday, Roseen Teare.

Picture Credits

a-above; b-below/bottom; c-centre; l-left; r-right; t-top

Works of art have been reproduced with the permission of the following copyright holders: *Wall Drawing 684A* June 1999 (Colour ink wash) Courtesy of the Estate of Sol Le Witt, First Installation Galerie Franck Schulte, Berlin First Drawn by Fransje Killaars, Roy Villevoye 44tr; *Turkey Pond* 1944 (Tempera on panel 32 1/4x 40 1/4") Courtesy of Farnsworth Art Museum, gift of Mr and Mrs Andrew Wyeth in memory of Walter Anderson 1995.2 52tc; *On the Bank of a River* 1904-5 Paul Cézanne Courtesy of RISD Museum of Art 48tr; *Madonna and Child with Saints* Sano di Pietro Courtesy of Smith College of Art Museum 48tl; *Portrait of My Daughters* 1907 Frank Benson Courtesy of Worcester Art Museum 44tl; *Rider Against Blue Hills* Maurice Brazil Prendergast Courtesy of Williams College Museum of Art 48br;

The publishers would like to thank the following individuals, companies and picture libraries for their kind permission to reproduce their photographs.

ALAMY IMAGES: Vicki Beaver 56tl; Michael Costolo 111tl; Danita Delimont/Jerry And Marcy Monkman 113tr; Kinn Deacon 138tc; Blaine Harrington III 71bl; Peter Arnold, Inc./ Phil Schermeister 16-7; Plus One Pix 1; RFR 70clb; Robert Harding Picture Library Ltd/Robert Francis 81cr; StockShot/Gary Pearl 54tr; Frank Vetere 100tl.

BOOTHBAY WHALE WATCH: 121tc.

CORBIS: Atlantide Phototravel/ Massimo Borchi 46-7; Bettmann 31br, 31cr, 31tr; Broudy/Donohue Photography 54tc; Comstock 113tl; Franz-Marc Frei 26-7, 65cla; Rick Friedman 73tr; Dave G. Houser 30tl; George H.H. Huey 135tl; Illustration Works/Antar Dayal 45cr; Hanan Isachar 27clb; Kelly-Mooney Photography 63r, 64tl; Layne Kennedy 119cl; Bob Krist 80cr; The Mariners' Museum 30cb; Francis G. Mayer 30cra; Smithsonian Institution 45tr (d); Dale C. Spartas 18-9; Sygma/Brooks Kraf 31bl; Visions of America/Joseph Sohm 106-7.

DORLING KINDERSLEY:
Courtesy of Dinosaur State Park, Connecticut 50c; Courtesy of Faneuil Hall Market Place, Boston 68cr; Courtesy of the Israel Sack Gallery, Hood Museum of Art, Dartmouth College, Hanover, NH 108tl; Courtesy of the Norman Rockwell Museum, Arlington, Vermont 45br; Courtesy of St Johnsbury Athenaeum Art Gallery, Vermont 101cl;

GETTY IMAGES: Aurora/Celin Serbo 126-7; Elsa 57r; Gallo Images/Travel Ink 30tc; Iconica/Skye Chalmers 54tl; The Image Bank/Johannes Kroemer 54bl; The Image Bank/Steve Dunwell 8-9; Douglas Mason 64br; Jim McIsaac 113tc; MPI 30tr; Photodisc/ Ben Bloom 17cra; Photonica/ Johannes Kroemer 2tr; Joe Robbins 3tl; Robert Harding World Imagery/ Guy Edwardes 4-5; Stone/Peter Vanderwarker 66-7.

MAINE LOBSTER FESTIVAL:
Courtesy The Herald-Gazette/www. villagesoup.com 64c; MAINE OFFICE OF TOURISM: 56bl, 57clb; Courtesy of the MUSEUM OF FINE ARTS, Boston: Egypt Exploration Fund 44ca.

NHDTTD: Craig Alness 56tc.

PHOTOLIBRARY: Visions LLC 36cra, 111r; PORTLAND SCHOONER COMPANY: 22cla, 121tl.

SALEM WITCH MUSEUM, Salem, Massachusetts:Tina Jordan 69tr.

TANGLEWOOD:73tl.

All other images are © Dorling Kindersley. For further information see www.dkimages.com.

Acknowledgements

Selected Index of Places